The World Ends at the County Line

A Guide to Writing Stories People Want and Need to Read

Stan McKinney

Acknowledgements

This book is dedicated
to my wife, Joan Cottongim McKinney,
and my daughter, Calen.
Without their help and support,
this book would not have been possible.

Copyright 2004 by Stan McKinney

All rights reserved.

ISBN 1-59196-631-0

Special thanks to the Central Kentucky News-Journal,
The Sentinel-News and Landmark Community Newspapers Inc. for
their support in writing this book
and for granting permission to use stories
I wrote in their employ.
Special thanks also to Heather Davis and Daniel Kemp.

All of the photos in this book were taken by the author, with the exception of the photo of Jackie Pierce on page 216 which was taken by Calen McKinney, the photo of the author on page 235 which was taken by Calen McKinney and the photo of the author on the back cover which was taken by Joan Cottongim McKinney.

Table of Contents
The World Ends at the County Line
A Guide to Writing Stories
People Want and Need to Read

Foreword
Know your community   7

It is essential for a reporter to know the community. You have to know what's important in your own neighborhood.

Chapter 1
General guidelines   11

As a reporter you will deal with all kinds of stories. Learn how to recognize what matters and what doesn't.

Chapter 2
Who cares?   22

It's impossible to write an interesting story if you don't know your audience. Hang out at Dairy Queen or Wal-Mart. That's how you'll learn about the folks who read your newspaper.

Chapter 3
Let's write a few leads   32

Using information you might gather as a reporter, let's write some basic leads.

Chapter 4
Add some details, and you have a story   48

After you've written the lead to a story, you start adding details. The most important details come first. Before you know it, you have a complete story.

Chapter 5
News affects people   **58**

News is the heart of any newspaper. Some papers, though, publish stories with little life in them. No matter what the topic might be, every story can be humanized. Think and write about what affects people.

Chapter 6
Features   **78**

Everyone has a story to tell. People like to read about interesting things people do. The trick is to make the stories interesting.

Chapter 7
Sports   **100**

Many people take sports seriously. Writers must too, even if they are not sports fans. All stories don't have to be about basketball, football or baseball. If you can write about people, you can write about sports.

Chapter 8
Obituaries   **111**

The inevitable conclusion to life is death. Some people's deaths, for many reasons, are more newsworthy than others. Some lives end tragically and unexpectedly. Such stories must be approached with compassion and sensitivity.

Chapter 9
Opinion writing   **121**

There are few reporters and editors who can resist offering their two cents worth. That, of course, is not permitted in news or other stories. Writing a column or editorial can let you get a lot off your chest. Strong opinion pieces are also popular with readers.

Chapter 10
Investigative stories   138
The "why" behind a story may often be unclear. There are many ways to get at the "truth" behind a story without weeks or months of investigation.

Chapter 11
Controversial stories   156
Sooner or later, something you write will disturb or offend someone. It's impossible to please all the people all the time.

Chapter 12
Public meetings, the courts   170
Public meetings, such as school boards and city councils, are often the "bread and butter" for many newspapers. So are trials and other court actions. Coverage does not have to be routine.

Chapter 13
Special events   188
Press conferences, celebrations, even trips to the Miss America Pageant, could be part of your beat. Many such events happen with advance notification. Some do not. You have to prepare the best that you can.

Chapter 14
Enjoy your job   203
Jimmy Buffett once sang, "If we weren't all crazy, we would all go insane." Being a reporter can sometimes be tough; it can also be fun. Enjoy the good times. They can help you forget the bad.

Chapter 15
A writer must write   211
If you want to be a reporter, you've got to write stories. Find a subject that interests you. Do some interviews. Write the story. Submit it to newspapers. Get your work noticed. That can help you land a job.

Chapter 16
Your turn,
identify the basic elements of these stories   219

Read these stories and determine the who, what, when, where, why, how and who cares of each. Also, what do you like about these stories, and what do you not like?

Appendix A   228

If you follow these guidelines, you should be able to remain in the good graces of your editor and/or readers.

Appendix B   231

Here are my thoughts on "your turn."

Appendix C   232

Reporters often must be photographers. It's not all that difficult to write and take photos.

About the author   234

Stan McKinney was a reporter, photographer and editor for more than 25 years. He has been a university professor since 1987.

Foreword

Know your community

How important is a water line to the residents of Caseyville, Ky.?

That's a question I faced on my first day as a reporter. It's a question I couldn't answer despite the fact I had a bachelor of science in journalism and was within six hours of completing my master's degree.

I was no longer in the classroom. At age 21, I was in the real world where people expected me to know the answers to real questions.

I had absolutely no idea how important treated water might be to Caseyville residents. Heck, I didn't even know how many people lived in Caseyville or where it was for that matter.

The question came up during the first fiscal court meeting I covered. And, that was during my first visit to Morganfield, Ky., the seat of government in Union County in far northwestern Kentucky.

I thought I had done well to find Morganfield, the courthouse and the room where fiscal court met.

When the discussion turned to a state grant for a water line to Caseyville, a small community in the western corner of Union County, I was venturing again into new territory. I had never really thought about where water comes from and didn't understand why everyone seemed to be so pleased that money had been approved for the line.

I gathered all of the information I could from the meeting, asked the judge a few questions and then headed back to Sturgis, Ky., about 15 miles or so down the road.

Sturgis is home to about 2,000 people as well as the Sturgis News. With the exception of Morganfield, Sturgis is the largest town in Union County.

It was Tuesday (I can't remember why I didn't start work on a Monday) and unbeknownst to me, the deadline for the weekly Sturgis News was fast approaching.

Since it was almost 5 p.m., I had thought about going back to the office, clocking out for the day, going home and coming back refreshed the next day to bang out something Caseyville residents would be proud to read.

My plans quickly changed.

The newspaper's typesetter was waiting for me at the front door. (It was 1975 and stories were still created on typewriters and then typeset on a Compugraphic, a massive machine once used by most newspapers to create neat, readable, justified type.)

The typesetter made it clear to me that she wanted to go home and couldn't do so until she had set my story for Wednesday's newspaper.

I stared at her, my notes and a typewriter that I had not yet had an opportunity to use.

Fortunately, the owner of the newspaper was still at the office. I quizzed him briefly about fiscal court, Caseyville and the water line. He made some suggestions. I incorporated them into my story.

I will never forget composing the story in my mind, typing the words on that manual typewriter with a faded ribbon and watching as the typesetter literally ripped each completed page from my hands.

There was no chance to read over my story before it was set. I was not able to check my spelling. I had to forget about tweaking my lead.

The typesetter was too anxious to go home. She wasn't waiting any longer than absolutely necessary. She was a veteran employee. I was as green as one could possibly be, and I didn't know how to use the Compugraphic.

I couldn't write as fast as she could type, so after completing one page, she was soon back to wait for the next. Somehow I managed to write a reasonably coherent story in about 30 minutes.

I realized I was in the real world where water lines and deadlines matter.

That was my introduction to some of the deadline pressures that are all too common in the newspaper business.

I later learned that Caseyville is a small community with a population of about 20 or so. Another couple hundred folks live in the area and would also benefit from the water line.

The water line, in fact, was a blessing to those residents. Wells and cisterns had been their only sources of water. Some of the wells often went dry. A few produced water that had a bad taste, bad smell or both.

There were serious questions about the impurities in the well water. Some of the water most likely wasn't safe for human consumption.

To the Caseyville residents, the grant for a water line was a BIG story.

Wouldn't it have been great to talk with some of those people?

An elderly couple who had used foul smelling water for drinking and bathing most of their lives probably could have given me some great quotes. A young couple just getting started and thinking about moving away from Caseyville because "good" water had not been available would also have been a good source.

What if an industry was now considering locating near the community because of the water line? Great source, right?

Time did not permit seeking out such sources for that first story. I had to make the best of the time I had. I've also learned much since them. People like to read about people, the challenges they face and how they meet them.

How important was the water line to the other residents of Union County? That's debatable. Certainly interest in the water line decreased the farther away from Caseyville one lived.

If the water line could have attracted a new industry, that possibly would have impacted many from a wide area. Jobs, after all, are an essential part of life.

Those nearby may have seen the grant as hope for their own water lines. Some may have once been in the same position and understood how critical the issue was to their friends and neighbors.

After all, they were all part of one community. They cared about each other and what affected one mattered to all of them.

That's the case in most communities. People care about the news that directly affects them or their friends and neighbors. That's understandable.

Hang out at Wal-Mart. Eat at Dairy Queen or McDonald's on occasion. Attend a Little League baseball game. Drive down Main Street on a Saturday night and see what cruising is really like.

Talk to the mechanic who changes your oil.

Attend church. Visit several churches and talk to different ministers and members of various congregations.

Drop by a local nursing home. Chat with the administrator and residents, if possible. Chat with your dentist, your doctor, your banker, everyone who provides some kind of service for you.

Go to a fiscal court or city council meeting even if that's not your beat. Visit your local schools. Make sure that at least a couple of times each year you visit every community in your county.

See and be seen.

Become involved in your community. Contrary to what many might believe, it is possible to join a civic club, coach a ball team, teach Sunday School, give blood and otherwise be involved without losing your objectivity.

Being involved makes you human. And that, I believe, makes you a better writer.

Learn what matters to those who read your newspaper. You'll find those issues also matter to you.

I wrote the majority of the stories you will be reading and discussing when I was the news editor of the Central Kentucky News-Journal in Campbellsville, Ky. A few, and they will be pointed out, were written by me as a reporter for The Sentinel-News in Shelbyville, Ky. and as a reporter for the Sturgis News.

Landmark Community Newspapers Inc. (LCNI) owns the Central Kentucky News-Journal and The Sentinel-News. LCNI is a division of Landmark Newspapers, based in Norfolk, Va., which owns newspapers, radio stations, TV stations, magazines, cable companies and specialty publications all across the country. It also owns The Weather Channel.

Landmark hires good people and gives them the freedom necessary to do their jobs.

Campbellsville is located almost exactly in the center of Kentucky. It is the center of government and commerce for Taylor County.

Shelbyville is located a short drive east of Louisville, Ky. It is the center of government and commerce for Shelby County. Shelbyville is also home to corporate headquarters for LCNI.

The Sturgis News, at the time of my employment, was owned by Bud and Ed Calman.

Everyone I worked for encouraged me to know my community and to be part of it. They taught me that knowing and caring about what's happening at home is essential if you are to be an effective community journalist.

For the most part, what happens across the county line really isn't important. There are, of course, exceptions to that. Really big stories such as war know no arbitrary political boundaries. The trick is to relate the big story to local folks. You have to bring the story home.

That's why I believe, as far as community newspapers are concerned, the world ends at the county line.

Chapter 1
General guidelines

Eons ago, when dinosaurs still ruled the planet and I was in college, I did manual labor during the summers.

OK, I'm not really that old. I just wanted to get your attention.

I actually did do manual labor during the summers when I was in college. One summer I hauled hay. One hour of such labor today would probably kill me, but that has nothing to do with the point I wish to make.

My boss that summer was a nice enough person. He, however, had a bit of a communication problem.

Simple writing is best

When giving instructions, this gentleman always took a moment and appeared to go into a trance before saying anything to my fellow laborers and me. After he regained consciousness, huge words with multiple syllables slowly spewed from his mouth.

My comrades and I often stared at each other and wondered what we had been told. Dictionaries are not standard issue for hay hauling crews. Thus, we had "a failure to communicate."

I now refer to the BIG words my former boss attempted to use as "$100 words." One hundred bucks is still a significant sum today for most people. For a college student in the 1970s, it was a small fortune.

Had my former boss used "quarter words" to communicate, I believe there would have been no communication problem and our work could have been completed much faster.

By the way, we were paid for each bale of hay we handled, not by the hour. Most people don't mind wasting a little time if they are paid to do it. We wanted to pick up those bales of hay instead of scratching our heads in an attempt to figure out what we had been told.

One of my former newspaper colleagues once told me that a good newspaper on occasion should use words that "send readers scrambling for their dictionaries." He believed that people could improve their vocabulary if the media challenged them once in awhile.

Any student who agrees with that probably would flunk my classes.

Why?

Let's get real here. How many people do you think really sit with a dictionary in hand as they read a newspaper? How many would take the time to find a dictionary if they encountered a word they didn't understand?

Few, if any.

People are busy. They have more important things to do than consult reference books when they read a newspaper.

I could argue that there has been a "dumbing down" of America. Broadcast news is short and to the point. Most newspapers are beginning to imitate their electronic counterparts. Stories are becoming shorter and simpler.

Like it or not, that's the trend.

I still hang onto the notion that newspapers can provide detail that television and radio cannot. What's the point, though, if no one wants that detail?

I'm not going to debate that point. That's for another book.

I do believe, though, that "quarter words" are better than "$100 words." I also believe that our writing should be designed to communicate information quickly and easily. People are not going to run for their dictionaries because you have chosen to use a word they don't understand.

That doesn't mean we write such things as "See Dick," "See Jane" or "See Dick and Jane."

We don't want to insult our readers. We also do not want to create stumbling blocks that would interfere with the communication process. Know your readers. Know their educational level. Use various software programs to determine what grade level on which you are writing and the average length of your sentences.

Vary your sentence length. Normally limit yourself to one idea per sentence.

Remember, you are not writing great literature. You are writing stories that the average person can comprehend. You are not writing to impress.

Remember that.

There are many types of stories

Much has been written about what is and what is not news. Most of us probably have at least a vague notion of how news, features, sports and columns differ. Some of us may not.

In each chapter, I will explore the differences in more detail.

What is an advertorial? What is a sports feature? What is a news feature?

Such writing exists, and understanding the difference can be difficult.

News is something that affects people

News has many definitions. It can be one or all of the following:
—It is a break from the ordinary.
—It is something that impacts many people.
—It is something that is important NOW.
—It is something that affects those who live in your community.
—It is something affecting well-known people.
—It involves conflict or controversy.

Most news stories are written in the inverted pyramid style – that is the most important facts are listed first, generally in the lead.

The lead is the first sentence or two of a story. It introduces the story and should grab readers' attention.

More about leads in a moment.

Details follow the lead in order of importance. That means the least important facts come last and, in theory, could be cut from the story for space or other reasons without affecting the overall meaning.

Taken to the extreme, if the lead is the only thing left of a news story, a reader should be able to get at least a basic idea of what happened.

The role of the editor

News also is what the editor says it is.

What does that mean?

Odds are as a reporter your story assignments will come from an editor. That editor most likely will also help shape your questions and your final story. He/she will also decide what editing must be done and where in the newspaper the story will be printed, if at all.

In short, an editor can kill a story before a word is written or bring to life a topic a reporter might not have wanted to write about in the first place.

Every news story of any significance affects people. Determine exactly how it affects people and precisely whom it affects. Once you've done that, write about those effects, ideally in those people's words.

The greater the magnitude of those effects and the larger the number of people involved, the more important and interesting the story is.

Other types of stories

The Kentucky Press Association sponsors an annual contest that honors the best newspaper writers in the state. The association classifies stories according to 12 categories.

News is broken down by the KPA into spot and general news. The KPA also has categories for features, columns, editorials, sports columns, sports stories, sports features, enterprise or analytical stories, investigative stories, on-going/extended coverage and business/agribusiness stories.

Let's look at those categories.

Spot news is something that happens without any prior notice and for which no advance planning is necessary. Accidents, fires, disasters, murders, etc. would all fall into that category.

General news incorporates such things as coverage of school board, fiscal court and city council meetings. It would also include coverage of press conferences, groundbreakings, etc., all of which are scheduled and permit some advance planning.

Coverage of public meetings is so important for small newspapers that a chapter will be devoted to the subject.

Feature stories are viewed by many as stories written primarily to entertain. They often resemble short stories. Feature stories are usually not written in inverted pyramid style.

I believe it is possible for feature stories to be written about newsworthy topics. A news feature, if you will, would be more detailed and perhaps focus more on an individual involved in an issue rather than the issue itself.

Features generally are not time dependent. That means they could be published virtually at any time with no loss in their value to readers. The exception would be a feature that contains items that are newsworthy.

A column is normally written by an individual and contains his or her observations or conclusions.

An editorial is usually the opinion of the newspaper as determined by an editorial board. A member of that board usually writes it. The board normally consists of representatives from the various departments of the newspaper.

A sports column is the opinion or observations of the writer regarding a sports topic.

A sports story sticks to the facts and describes what happened or didn't happen during a sporting event.

A sports feature likely would focus on an individual and include details a story normally wouldn't. It's usually more detailed and, perhaps, more entertaining.

Enterprise involves the reporter getting out and digging up something new. It requires more than routine effort. An analytical story attempts to answer the why and how, something many news stories usually just touch on because of time limitations.

Thus, an enterprise or analytical story requires much more work and time than most stories and is usually original.

An investigative story also involves digging deep into an issue and trying to determine how or why something happened. It might involve hours of searching through files, tracking down sources or much, much more.

You might also justifiably wonder how this category differs from enterprise or analytical.

Some stories seem to go on forever. That doesn't necessarily mean they are boring. When Fruit of the Loom closed in Campbellsville in late 1997, for example, it took months for all of the effects to be felt. One could even argue they are still being felt today.

It took many stories to bring to light the full impact of the plant's closing. That's on-going/extended coverage.

Business/agribusiness stories should be self-explanatory. They are stories about business or farms. Such stories probably could also be classified as features or news.

KPA offers the business/agribusiness category to give more writers an opportunity to win an award.

All of these categories, it could be argued, represent a form of news. After all, news is something someone has not heard about, something that matters.

All stories, in my opinion, must make it clear as to how people are affected.

Still other categories

I've already mentioned that a story can be both news and feature. That will be explained in more detail in another chapter.

There are some other types of stories that you may also encounter.

Let's first talk about special sections. All newspapers print them. Most reporters hate them.

I'm talking about special sections devoted to topics such as gardening, June weddings, winter car care and the like.

While some of these sections may be interesting and even useful, they are produced for one reason – to make money. Let's not forget that a newspaper is a business and must make a profit.

A newspaper that doesn't make a profit won't last long. That directly affects reporters.

Making a profit, though, doesn't have to mean selling your soul.

I believe that a credible, objective newspaper attracts and keeps readers. In turn, a newspaper with a large number of readers attracts advertisers who pay good money to spread their messages.

Advertisers may at times get angry with newspapers for printing material they would rather not see and might even pull their ads for awhile.

If the ad was truly doing something for the advertiser, the newspaper won't be the only one to suffer. I believe the advertiser will ultimately come back. The advertiser may continue to dislike the paper but will continue advertising because to not do so would affect his business.

Back to my point.

Let's say you are doing a story about lawn care. There are many interested in the topic, including me.

Within your coverage area there are five lawn care professionals. Three of them advertise in the special section. Two do not.

Who are you going to talk with for your story? If you talk to the two who do not advertise, there are two problems. Those two may believe there was never any reason to advertise because the story provided them with free publicity.

The three who did advertise might not do so again because those who didn't spend any money were included in the story.

Many newspapers will not include those who did not advertise as sources for such special sections. That's why some refer to these kinds of stories as advertorial – a combination of ads and editorial content.

I'm not going to debate the ethics of writing these types of stories. As a reporter you simply might not have a choice.

I am also aware of at least one newspaper that promises stories to those who advertise. A good friend of mine while in college interviewed for a job at such a paper.

Looking at that paper was an eye-opening experience. On one

page would be an ad for a company. On the next page would be a story about that company. I only had to wonder what the readers of that newspaper thought.

Promising stories in exchange for ads, in my opinion, is more than unethical. It is an abomination.

What do readers want?

Readers, as a whole, are not that demanding. They want news that is relevant and meaningful. They want it to be fresh, well written, interesting and accurate.

That means spelling all names correctly. I have found readers can forgive a lot, but most would never accept their names being misspelled.

Readers want us to get all of the facts and figures correct. They want us to leave out our opinions unless we are writing a column or editorial.

Readers want us to be fair and compassionate. They want us to realize that stories can embarrass and harm people. They want us to tell them what they need to know. Sometimes they also want us to entertain them.

They want to be able to reach us if necessary. They want to know who we are and understand why we do what we do. Columns, I believe, can help us accomplish that.

Readers want us to get it right. And we should.

The search for truth

Many reporters will tell you that they got into journalism to report the truth or to help make their community a better place.

That's all well, good and very noble.

But what exactly is truth?

Usually when I talk about truth in class, I put the word in quotation marks. "Truth" can be many things to many people.

Who's telling the truth if two eyewitnesses at an accident tell vastly different stories? Who's telling the truth if an elected official says he didn't take a bribe but a source, who has no written or other proof, says he did?

Some people lie. Some people distort the facts for their own purposes. Some people use the media. That's just the way it is.

There are those who believe high officials in the U.S. government were actually responsible for the attacks against America on Sept. 11, 2001. Somewhere in my vast collection of publications I have a pamphlet that goes into great detail to explain why those officials staged the attacks for their own personal gain.

Is this pamphlet telling the truth?

Most people would think not.

I did a story once about several families who live in one community. Those on one side of the road refer to their community as Lemmon's Bend. Those on the other side of the road call it Lemon's Bend. The official county map lists the community as Lemmon Bend.

Who's right?

One of my bosses over the years told me "perception is reality." People sometimes believe what they want to believe and no one and nothing, even the truth, can change that.

All you can do is report the truth to the best of your ability. That means including conflicting viewpoints and as many sides of a story as possible.

Stories could have one, two or 2,000 sides. Some may also not deserve as much coverage as others. If 10,000 people believe one thing and one person believes something else, do both viewpoints demand equal space?

Probably not.

Be as fair and objective as possible.

Realize that you may be offended by what some people tell you. Treat those who do offend you or who challenge your own beliefs with respect. Show no favoritism. Question everything.

Stand up for your readers. Ask the questions they would if they had the chance.

Using quotes

Quotes can transform a dull story into an interesting one. Tell stories through your readers' words when possible.

Some people, quite frankly, are not that interesting. Good writing is more than a series of quotes and some punctuation marks. If something isn't worth quoting or can be said in a simpler manner, paraphrase.

Quote marks, to me, indicate the *exact* words a person said. Quotes are what the readers would have heard had they been there.

Some might argue that the only way to get accurate quotes is to use a tape recorder. I hate tape recorders. They force a writer to go back and listen to a conversation again. Notes permit you to edit as you go and to quickly find details for a story.

It is possible to take notes precise enough to accurately quote someone. Practice that skill.

What do you quote?

Something quotable. That means use the speakers' own words when they best convey the message.

Let me give you an example.

Let's say you are writing a story about a school system that did poorly on statewide tests and faces possible state sanctions. You interview the school superintendent about the situation and he replies with this: "We ain't got no problem."

That quote is not only quotable, it's your lead, your story and probably even your headline. A reporter who would not use that quote, in my opinion, is not worthy of the title.

Sure, the superintendent, school board and maybe even some members of the general public might be upset and blame the newspaper for embarrassing them. That's their problem.

The statement is indicative of a much larger problem and is the essence of the story. A reporter has an obligation to use it.

Most quotes won't be that good. But many people will tell their own stories much better in their own words than any writer ever could. Look for those quotes. You'll find them.

Writing the lead

The lead, I believe, is the most important part of any story. It must grab the reader and entice him to read further. It must tell the reader why he should care about the story and why he must read it.

Journalists have understood for years that the lead should answer all basic questions – who, what, when, where, why and how.

Those five Ws and H will be discussed in detail for every story in this book. Another important W, who cares, will also be discussed at length.

It's difficult to say exactly at what point in the writing process a lead is born. You might have an idea for a lead as the story idea is taking shape.

The answer to a single question might result in the lead. It might take a bit of poring over your notes to determine what's most important and of most importance. Once that lead is written, though, I believe most stories fall into place.

The next most important information follows. Wrap up the story in some way and you're finished.

Sounds easy, doesn't it?

For some, writing is easier than others. It can be a chore, but hopefully it can become a labor of love.

How long should a lead be?

Many books I've read suggest that a lead should be no more than 29 words. I've also seen 19 words listed as a maximum. I believe a lead should be as short as possible. In my opinion, 29 words are probably too many.

One of my former bosses subscribed to what he called the mini-skirt theory. Forgive me if this sounds sexist. He believed a story should be long enough to cover the subject but short enough to keep your interest – just like a mini-skirt.

Story length

Over the years, many reporters and students have quizzed me about story length.

My response is very simple. A story should be as long as it needs to be.

That's not a flippant answer. Stories must be complete. They are complete when all questions are answered.

Thus, stories set their own length. This is where the mini-skirt theory comes into play.

A very simple subject most likely will result in a short story. A complicated story that has many points of view most likely will be longer.

Think about the subject. Imagine every possible question someone might ask. If you've answered all of those, the story is as long as it needs to be. If there are questions that readers will have and they haven't been answered, you haven't written enough.

Features tend to be longer than news stories.

In general, a brief, simple story can probably be written in a paragraph or two, a half page at most. Stories of some significance probably require a minimum of two pages, perhaps three. At four pages, a story is starting to get long.

Features most likely will be three to four pages in length.

These are guidelines only. Every story is different.

If a story is too long, consider writing two stories. There's no law, for example, that requires reporters to write only one story about a public meeting or other matter. I have written as many as five stories from one meeting.

A series is also possible, if the amount of information justifies it.

Remember, there's only so much information a person wants to take in at one time.

Attribution

Only columns and editorials can be written without attribution. If you're quoting something someone said or commenting on something from a source, attribution is necessary even for them.

A reporter is a conduit for information, never a source.

It is important that the reader know who the sources are for all stories. That affects credibility. Identify who said what. Tell us who complained, asked for something or otherwise provided the information for a story.

As far as I'm concerned, "said" is the only word to use when attributing information. Charged, claimed, hinted, laughed, smiled, suggested and all of those other "clever" words add meaning to a story. That meaning may very well introduce bias into a story. "Said" adds no meaning.

This book cannot possibly answer all questions one might have about writing for a newspaper. There are issues regarding the law, grammar, style, covering the courts, etc. that a reporter must also know.

The focus of this book is the writing process. And that will be explained by looking at a number of stories and discussing how and why they were written.

Chapter 2

Who cares?

The first step in writing a story – any story – is to determine the potential audience. Will it interest or affect virtually every reader? Will it be of interest or importance to most? Or will it be of interest or importance to only a few?

Obviously, if only the source and writer care about the story, it isn't much of a story.

In short, before asking a single question, taking any notes, or even thinking about a lead, ask yourself who cares about this story?

If you can't answer that question, you're not ready to begin writing.

Some writers, unfortunately, bore people to death in the first paragraph or two. Their mothers might read a few such stories, but I wouldn't count on that. Certainly, careers can't be built with the mothers of reporters as the only audience.

I've known students and reporters who wrote the most boring leads imaginable and were surprised that few actually read far enough to learn why they should have cared. A few admitted to me that they wouldn't have read the stories themselves.

How then do we make stories interesting?

First of all, people like to read about things that happen to people.

Let me repeat that. People like to read about things that happen to people.

(Forgive the grammar in the following. I'm butchering the English language for the purpose of emphasis.)

Fiscal court isn't people. Taylor County Magistrate Bobby Kirtley is people and what he had to say quite often was interesting, frustrating and of consequence to many. More about him later.

A school board isn't people. Campbellsville Superintendent Dave Fryrear is people and the reasons he supported a utility tax to keep the school system financially sound greatly affected the community. His belief that the tax was the only way to save the school system was of importance.

A tax rate isn't people. Citizen John Smith, already dealing with a tight budget, who as a result of a new tax must pay an additional three cents on every dollar of his utility bills, is of interest.

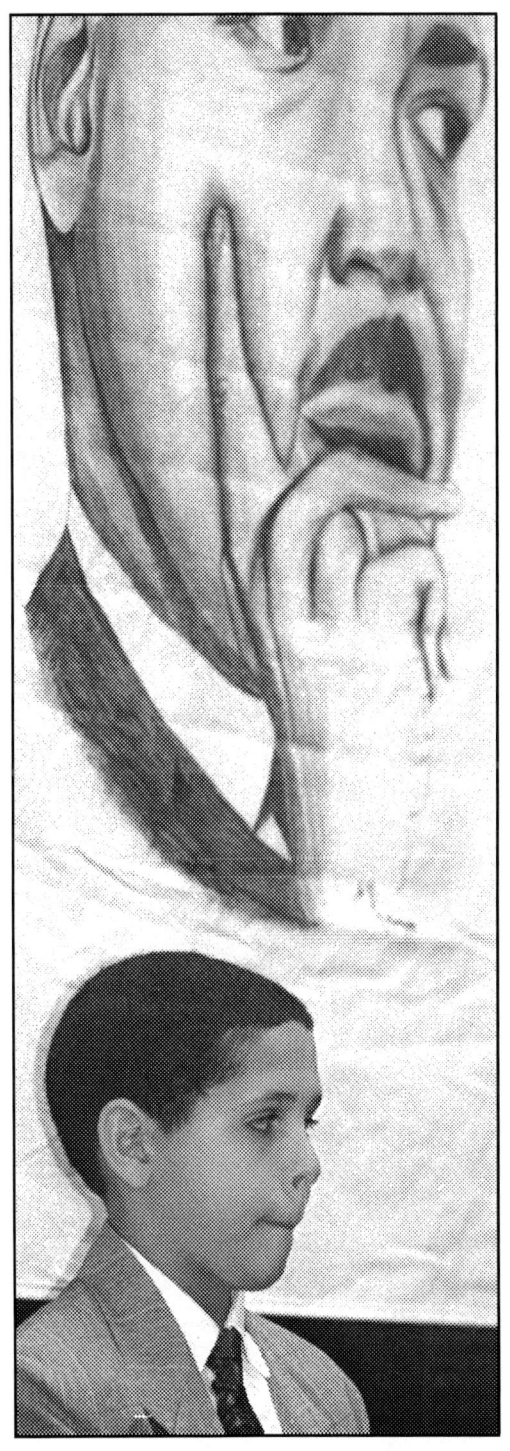

You must look in order to see

Could you write a story based on what you see in this photo?

The large-scale drawing is of Dr. Martin Luther King Jr.

The little boy was one of several hundred attending a celebration honoring the slain civil rights leader's birthday.

Could you talk about Dr. King's dream, the little boy's dream and how the dream has changed?

There's a story here. All you have to do is see it, ask the right questions and then write it.

That citizen's story makes for good reading. It's also one most people can relate to on a personal level.

Septic tanks isn't people. Citizen Alice Jones who can't walk in her back yard or hang out clothes to dry because of the stench from raw sewage is. Again, her story is the kind people like to read and can understand.

Tell stories through people. Show how the news affects local residents where they live, work and play.

Before looking at several stories and discussing why and how they were written, let's consider something else.

As a reporter for the Sturgis News and The Sentinel-News, it was important for me to know the people who called each of those communities home.

As news editor for the Central Kentucky News-Journal from 1980 to 2000, it was essential for me to know its audience. After all, how can one write stories and direct others who write stories without a clear understanding of what matters to your audience?

That means knowing as much as possible about your community. That includes many demographics such as age, religion, educational level, etc. You can't stop there, though. You must know the faces of your readers.

Since the majority of the stories we will discuss were written for the Central Kentucky News-Journal, I'm going to discuss the community in some detail. Again, find out all you can about your community before asking one question or writing one story.

The Central Kentucky News-Journal is the only local paper that serves Campbellsville, the seat of government for Taylor County.

By the way, you need to know at least the general history of your community. That knowledge WILL be useful at some point in time.

The average reader of the Central Kentucky News-Journal is middle-aged, has an 11th grade education and an income of about $25,000. The circulation of the newspaper is about 7,000.

The newspaper is published each Monday and Thursday.

You can't know what you need to know by only going to the office each day.

You must shop at Wal-Mart. You must frequent the small mom and pop businesses that are still open. Even if you don't like coffee, you simply must spend some time hanging around the local watering hole. You must go where the people are.

It's at places such as these that you find out about the people who make up your community. That's information you must have before you can write stories about which your community cares.

You must find out if your readers prefer city ham or country ham. You must learn the difference if you don't already know.

It's good to know if they cheer for the Kentucky Wildcats or the Louisville Cardinals. (Most in Taylor County bleed Kentucky Blue though many do see Cardinal Red.)

There are more than 100 churches in Taylor County. That means religion is important and at times warrants front page coverage.

Drive around the community. Learn where things are. Make it your home.

I was asked in the summer of 2001 to write a story about Campbellsville for Kentucky Monthly magazine. While I knew most of the information that ultimately was included in the story, I had to have real, live sources. I also had to have exact figures, not some of the approximations I had in my head for things such as population.

The mayor was a logical source. So was the head of the industrial development authority. Many other facts and figures came from the Chamber of Commerce, tourism brochures and the like.

The story details what Campbellsville was, is and may be in the future. It follows:

Campbellsville
Economic trials have made it stronger

Paul Osborne says there's no place he would rather live than Campbellsville.

Given the fact that Osborne is the mayor of Campbellsville, such a statement probably isn't surprising. He's not just bragging about the community of 10,498 located in the exact center of the state and he's not just practicing good public relations.

Osborne truly wouldn't want to live anywhere else.

"I love the people here and their neighborly approach to things," Osborne said. "The people are friendly and work together as a team."

The resolve of Campbellsville citizens was tested a couple of years ago when Fruit of the Loom and later Batesville Casket Co. announced they were leaving town. Together, the two employed more than 4,000 people.

The announcements initially devastated Campbellsville

and Taylor County. The citizens rallied together and made some tough decisions. At a time when additional government expenditures might have seemed unwise to some, city and county governments jointly stepped up their industrial recruitment efforts. With the help of state and federal governments, economic incentives were offered to a variety of new industries.

Those efforts have reaped great benefits.

The information super highway, not asphalt, has brought many industries and customers to town in recent years, Osborne said.

Amazon.com, for example, opened a major distribution center and fills orders placed all over the world through the Internet.

Rosenbluth International bought out an existing travel agency and training academy, expanded and began handling corporate travel for clients all over the world. It relies on the World Wide Web.

Frost-Arnett Co. went online and provides collection services and third-party billing for companies all over the country.

But companies such as Amazon.com need real asphalt to deliver the goods.

With funding from the state and federal governments, highway access from the west is being greatly improved. That, Osborne said, should open up the area even more for manufacturers and should also be an asset for those who take orders through the Internet but rely on roads to deliver.

Manufacturers have also responded positively to Campbellsville's courtship:

—Campbellsville Apparel bought an empty building and started producing a variety of garments including T-shirts for various customers like Fruit of the Loom and the U.S. Army.

—Brentwood International moved to Campbellsville from Louisville. The company produces gift wrap and distributes a variety of products.

—Murakami Manufacturing USA is gearing up to produce rear-view mirrors for a variety of vehicles. The company hopes to be in production this month.

—Fleetwood Travel Trailers of Kentucky purchased a spec building and began producing a new product line.

—Airguard purchased the former Batesville Casket Co. site and is manufacturing air filters.

The community's largest employer is Cox Interior, which manufactures hardwood moldings, trim, stair parts, interior doors and mantels. Other industries produce church steeples, cupolas, awnings and other aluminum and steel products, a variety of wood products, cherry furniture, screen-printing, and textile machinery.

"We are more diversified now than ever," Osborne said.

"Many of the jobs we have added are 21st century jobs. We have begun to think globally."

Farming is also important to the area, with tobacco and corn among the principle crops.

In many ways, the location of Campbellsville, the Taylor County seat, is ideal. It is almost equally distanced from Louisville, Lexington and Bowling Green. An interstate highway, however, doesn't run near the city or Taylor County, for that matter.

Campbellsville's location also makes it easy for citizens to sample big-city life while retreating easily to a quieter way of life.

Green River Lake State Park, located only a few miles outside the city limits, attracts 1.2 million visitors each year. The 8,200-acre lake offers a variety of campgrounds, boat ramps, sandy beaches, marinas and other facilities for hiking and horseback riding, among many things.

The natural beauty of the lake attracted the eye of Wendy's founder Dave Thomas, a member of the board for the Tim Horton Children's Foundation of Canada. The foundation recently opened its first camp in the United States on a 50-acre site overlooking Green River Lake.

"We had seen seven different sites in the states," said Keith Publicover, executive director of the foundation.

"This site is just beautiful."

The camp provides an opportunity for children from Canada to visit the United States. The foundation will also fly youngsters from central Kentucky to camp in Canada on an exchange basis.

Numerous historical sites also draw visitors each year. The Atkinson-Griffin Log Structure, adjacent to the Green River Lake Information Center, was built in 1840 and served as a Confederate hospital during the Civil War.

Also near the lake is the Tebbs Bend Battleground and trail. On the site, 200 Union soldiers defended the crossing at Green River against Morgan's advance. Though outnumbered four to one, the Union troops successfully slowed Morgan and his men during the Great Raid.

Other sites on the National Register of Historic Places include Clay Hill, a house built by slaves in 1835, and the Jacob Hiestand House, built in 1832.

The Jacob Hiestand House, one of only 12 German stone houses in the state and one of only two still standing, has been restored and is open to the public.

There are also numerous antique shops in the area. Several craftsmen call the community home, among them Roger Blair, a woodcarver who was featured in former Kentucky first lady Phyllis George's book on Kentucky craftspeople.

During the summer, Green River Lake hosts a gathering of Corvettes and crafters. The Green River Lake Arts and Crafts Festival, set for the third Saturday in July, features rare and unusual Corvettes in competition for numerous awards.

Craftspeople will also have items on display and for sale.

Campbellsville is home to one of the largest Fourth of July celebrations in the state.

The parade, which begins at 10 a.m. on July 4, often lasts an hour and a half. It attracts many state officials, including the governor.

The celebration also features a car show, tractor show, tractor pull, Big Wheel race for the kids, displays, craft items for sale, lots of food and a large fireworks show.

All are free.

Education is also of great importance to Campbellsville and Taylor County, Osborne said. He said Campbellsville University is invaluable to the community and has helped lead it into the future.

A technology training center is scheduled to open this fall on the campus of the private university affiliated with the Kentucky Baptist Convention and founded in 1906.

Campbellsville University has an enrollment of 1,600 and is listed in U.S. *News & World Report's* "America's Best Colleges" as one of the top Southern liberal arts colleges, and in *Kaplan/Newsweek's* College Catalog 2001 as a hidden treasure and a school that gives students individual attention from faculty.

U.S. Sen. Mitch McConnell helped secure a $2 million grant for the training center and during groundbreaking ceremonies last year said it will help the area better position itself technology-wise for the future.

The center will say to the world of business and industry that Campbellsville, Taylor County and Campbellsville University are serious about creating a new climate for industry and business, said John Chowning, a university vice president and chairman of the Campbellsville-Taylor County Industrial Development Authority.

A quality labor force, Chowning said, is one of the community's best selling points. He said a central location, much improved highway access, the university, Green River Lake and an affordable cost of living make the community the perfect place to live.

Osborne is so much at home that he hopes to encourage others to move to Campbellsville. Efforts are under way to get state certification as an ideal retirement community.

"I'm very hopeful that others will also recognize what a great place Campbellsville is to live," Osborne said.

A look at the basics
Who
The who of this story is the people of Campbellsville.

It can also be any community that ever faced a major challenge to its very existence. Who couldn't identify with that?

What
The what is how the community has worked together to survive. It is also the very essence of the community that makes it home to so many people and attracts so many visitors.

When
This story focuses on the now, by detailing how the recent challenges of the past were faced and it also looks to the future as the people of Campbellsville look forward.

Where
It's a small community, that could be one of many places in this country, faced with massive layoffs but a strong will to survive.

Why
That strong will answers the why of this story. People who are determined can do anything. The story touches on what could have hap-

pened had the community done nothing. It details why the community was able to succeed when others might have failed.

How

The how is addressed through the steps taken to lure new industries to the area as well as diversification which should eliminate such a devastating blow in the future. It's also addressed by the love residents have for the area.

Who cares

Anyone who lives in the area should care. Anyone who has ever lost a job should care. So should anyone who has ever lived in a small community and understands why residents feel such a strong bond.

Sources

The information for this story came from Campbellsville Mayor Paul Osborne; Keith Publicover, executive director of the Tim Horton Children's Foundation of Canada; John Chowning, chairman of the Campbellsville/Taylor County Industrial Development Authority; and the Campbellsville/Taylor County Chamber of Commerce.

Etc.

All of the interviews were done by telephone. There's no way a trip to Canada to talk in person with the chairman of the Tim Horton's Foundation could be justified when a short telephone call provided all the information necessary.

Talking with the others in person also would have taken much more time and simply was not necessary.

Working a few minutes here and there, it took about a week to gather all of the information. Writing the story took about two hours with another hour or so for editing.

This story provided an overview of the community. There were also space constraints for the magazine which serves a wide audience. In this instance, a general, overall story is what was needed.

Know your community

Know how most people earn their living. Know what kinds of food most like to eat when they go out for the evening. Know what kind of movies are most popular at the local theater.

Know what teams the locals cheer for on game day. Know what crops, those that are legal and illegal, generate the most money.

Know the police officers, the firefighters and those who can pry you out of a wrecked car and administer life-saving medical care. Know who the local ministers are, what the predominant religions are and how many flavors of Baptists there are in the community.

Know what matters to the people who call your community home. Care about them.

If you do all of this, your writing will show it.

Chapter 3

Let's write a few leads

Before we look at a variety of stories that fall into numerous categories and discuss the basics of each, let's study a few leads. Remember to consider the who, what, when, where, why and how for each. Also ask yourself who would care about the story.

Keep in mind that there very easily could be more than one who, what, when, where or why for each. Decide which of those is most important to your readers.

Read the information for each story carefully and jot down the basics. Sort through those basics and then write a lead for each.

At the end of this chapter, you will find the leads I believe are best for each of the four stories. You'll also find a discussion of why I believe they are best.

1. The following are the basic facts for a story to appear in Thursday's edition of The Sentinel-News in Shelbyville.

—The zoning commission met Tuesday night of the same week.

—The six commissioners were present as were 12 developers, four engineers, two members of the press and three "ordinary" citizens who didn't say a word during the meeting.

—Final approval was given to a subdivision that has been discussed for the past six months. The subdivision will contain 12 houses.

—The commission agreed to move next month's meeting from the fire station to the courthouse because of renovations.

—Commissioners answered questions from two developers regarding a new application form for those requesting building permits.

—The chairman of the commission read a report from the health department. A new regulation requires that septic tanks be permitted from now on only on lots of five acres or more in subdivisions. Most homes outside the city limits rely on septic tanks.

—There was no reaction from anyone regarding the new regulation.

—The commission adjourned with no further business and with no comments from anyone.

List the who, what, when, where, why, how and who cares for this story.

What is the most important part of this story? What is the least important?

Do you include everything?

Do you need additional information?

Write the lead to the best of your ability with the information you have.

2. It's Monday night and you are at a Campbellsville Board of Education meeting. You will be writing the story on Tuesday and it will be in Thursday's Central Kentucky News-Journal. There are more details for this lead than the previous exercise.

—After calling the roll, reading the treasurer's report and taking attendance, the superintendent asks if any member of the public would like to speak before the board takes up the items on the agenda.

—No one speaks.

—After approving financial reports, hearing about a progress report on construction of an elementary school that has just begun and is scheduled for completion within six months, the superintendent begins talking about taxes.

—Taxes must go up, the superintendent, Sam Smith, says if the school system is to pay for the school and cover all its bills.

—The superintendent said he has studied the problem with various financial experts and a 5 percent increase in taxes is necessary. The school is needed, he said, because of increased enrollment and crowded conditions in the existing elementary school.

—"We don't have a choice," Smith said.

—He said a hearing is set for Friday at 6 p.m. to discuss the tax and the school system's needs. The tax can be levied by the school board, he said, but if voters object and enough sign a petition the question would be on the ballot in May.

—"I hope we can convince people of the need and no one will object to the tax," Smith said.

—The average tax bill for city school district residents is $150 per year. A 5 percent increase would cost the average taxpayer $7.50 more per year.

List the who, what, when, where, why, how and who cares for this story.

What is the most important part of this story? What is the least important?

Do you include everything?

Do you need additional information?

Write the lead to the best of your ability with the information you have.

3. Write a lead based on the following:

—You just got back from a meeting of the board that oversees the Campbellsville Fourth of July Celebration. It is Thursday, June 10.

—This year's celebration won't be on the Fourth of July since the holiday falls on Sunday. Instead, in keeping with the board's policy, the celebration will be Monday, July 5. That's the day most businesses will close for the holiday.

—The annual parade on Main Street will begin the celebration at 10 a.m. The Grand Marshal will be Donna Wise, head coach of the women's basketball team at Campbellsville University. Earlier this year, she earned her 600th victory, something few coaches anywhere in the country can claim.

—The annual car show sponsored by the Tri-County Car Club will be at Campbellsville University instead of Miller Park.

—The board discussed at length the fact a major donor has withdrawn his annual contribution. That means the board is $5,000 short of enough money to pay for the fireworks show that always ends the celebration.

—Ten of the 12 members of the board were at the meeting.

—Eight members of the 10 present believe the fireworks show must be canceled. Seven believe the best thing to do is call off the entire celebration.

—The board is appointed by Campbellsville City Council but receives no government funding.

—The board, after much discussion, agreed to appeal to the public for donations. The board also said if the $5,000 needed cannot be raised by June 21, there will be no fireworks show.

—June 21 is the last day fireworks can be ordered in time for the celebration.

—The story you are writing will appear in the Monday, June 14 newspaper.

List the who, what, when, where, why, how and who cares for this story.

What is the most important part of this story? What is the least important?

Do you include everything?

Do you need additional information?

Write the lead to the best of your ability with the information you have.

4. Write a lead based on the following information for a Monday edition of The Sentinel-News in Shelbyville.

—The Centenary United Methodist Church has a new minister.

—No one in the community knows much about him. He has not yet moved to Shelbyville but you were able to interview him while he was in town to conclude the purchase of a home.

—The minister's name is Harold Smith.

—Smith is from Vine Grove, Ky. where he was minister at First United Methodist Church for 10 years. He is 45 years old, has a wife, Joan, and two daughters, Amy and Sallie.

—The Centenary United Methodist Church burned five weeks ago. Several stories have already detailed that. Smith was called as minister two weeks ago. The previous minister retired three months ago.

—Services are being conducted in the Shelbyville Fire Station until the church can be rebuilt. Smith has made numerous trips to town to meet with church elders and plan the necessary work.

—Everyone in town was shocked by the disaster which was ruled as arson. Many, including Smith, have called the burning of the church a tragedy.

—Smith has found himself tested as a minister though he does not yet live in Shelbyville. He will be moving to town two weeks from now.

List the who, what, when, where, why, how and who cares for this story.

What is the most important part of this story? What is the least important?

Do you include everything?

Do you need additional information?

Write the lead to the best of your ability with the information you have.

What should be in your leads?

1. Zoning commissions may sound boring, and sometimes they are. Such commissions also make decisions that greatly affect people's lives. This story affected many people. Do you know why?

Let's look at the basics. After that, we'll determine what's most important.

Who

In this category a reporter could place the six zoning commissioners, 12 developers, four engineers, two members of the press, three "ordinary" citizens, the chairman of the zoning commission and even the health department.

Who is most important? Let's look at all the elements before deciding which is most important and deserves the most emphasis.

What

It's a meeting of the zoning commission. It's final approval of a subdivision with 12 houses. It's a change in meeting locations. It's a new application form for building permits. It's a new regulation regarding the use of septic tanks in subdivisions.

When

It's Tuesday night. It's final approval for a subdivision. It's the beginning of a new application form. It's also the beginning of new rules regarding septic tanks.

Where

A couple of items fall into this category. The location of the next meeting would fit. So would the subdivision that received final approval. How about the requirement that septic tanks from now on may only be used in subdivisions with lots of five acres or more each? That also fits the category of where, doesn't it?

Why

Again, a couple of items could fall into this category. The move to a temporary location for the next meeting would. So would the reasons for a new application form and the final approval of the subdivision with 12 houses. The health department ruling regarding septic tanks would too, though we probably would want to know more.

How

We know that renovations will force the zoning commission to move its next meeting. We don't know how approval of a subdivision with 12 houses will affect the community. Is there a tremendous need for housing? Will 12 houses make much difference?

Some additional questions probably should be asked.

How will a new application form for building permits affect anyone? Is it just additional paperwork or is it a major issue? Again, we need to ask more questions.

How about the new five-acre rule regarding septic tanks in subdivisions? How will that affect people buying homes? Again, we need more information, but think for a moment here. Most homes in the county rely on septic tanks. Why? We need to ask some questions. But doesn't it appear that those building homes in subdivisions outside the city limits from now on must purchase at least five acres?

If you haven't figured it out by now, the five-acre rule is the most important part of the story. It must be emphasized in the lead.

Most homes in subdivisions are built on much smaller pieces of land.

Consider the consequences. Larger lots cost more. Larger lots also mean fewer homes. How will that affect the demand for housing?

Will housing costs increase because lots must be larger AND because fewer homes can now be built? Ask these questions of developers, real estate agents, bankers, builders and average citizens.

Homes built on lots smaller than five acres had to have their own sewage treatment systems. That's expensive — much more expensive, in fact, than a septic tank or five acres of land. Extending municipal sewers into all areas of the county also would be expensive. The impact of the five-acre rule would be tremendous.

This, by the way, is a real story. The cost of an average home in Shelby County did increase. Ultimately, a new tax was passed and sewer lines were extended into the county to eliminate the need for septic tanks.

At some point, you also would need to ask why five-acre lots were required if septic tanks were being used. The answer was fairly simple. The soil in most of the county wasn't suitable for septic tanks. If you've ever lived in a home with an improperly functioning septic tank, you know the problem.

If you don't know what a septic tank is, you would have quite a bit of basic research to do.

Who cares

Anyone planning to build a home certainly would. So would developers, real estate agents and all those others already mentioned. Their lives and businesses changed because of this rule.

The lead for this story should be something similar to this:

> Homes in Shelby County will cost more and fewer can be built because of a new health department regulation limiting the use of septic tanks.

That lead summarizes the most important information. Notice it does not mention the zoning commission.

The fact the ruling was discussed during the zoning commission meeting does not have to be in the lead. It probably needs to be in the story but can be much farther down.

I remember listening to all of the items discussed during the commission and considering them to be fairly routine.

The five-acre rule caught my attention, and I thought it was probably significant.

The fact no one commented on the new rule shook me a bit. I wondered why I thought it was significant if no one else even had any comment.

After the meeting I asked several questions. I quickly determined I was correct. Why no one commented on the new regulation during the meeting I will never know.

Time was short for this story. It was Tuesday night and my story for the Thursday edition of The Sentinel-News had to be ready by 10 a.m. Wednesday.

There wasn't time to interview everyone I would have liked for the story. I had to get what information I could from as many different people as possible and write my story.

There was time later for additional stories with more details.

Since this is a real story, let's look at the rest of it:

New rule will limit home building

Septic tanks will no longer be allowed in subdivisions with lots smaller than five acres following the passage of stricter regulations by the Shelby County Board of Health.

Such subdivisions under the new regulations must have a central sewage system or must connect to an existing, approved sewage system.

"I think it is going to slow down development in the county," said Horace Brown, a local engineer.

Brown said there are some alternatives to septic tanks but all are costly. Most developers and builders, he said, will probably decide to build only on lots of five acres or more and continue using septic tanks.

"That's going to mean the cost of buying a home will increase several thousand dollars," Brown said. "The number of homes that can be built will also decrease. That will mean higher prices, too."

The new regulations were discussed at last Tuesday's meeting of the Triple S Planning and Zoning Commission which was well attended by local engineers and developers.

"I'm surprised no one fainted," said Vic Brizendine, attorney for the zoning commission.

Edwin Hall, chairman of the commission, said the board of health was responsible for the new regulations. The commission, he said, only learned of them Tuesday.

The regulations also call for changes in percolation tests.

(A percolation test measures the ability of the ground to absorb water.)

The board of health's new regulations require minimum seepage to be one and one-half inches per half hour. During June, July, August and September, the rate must be two inches.

Previous regulations required a minimum seepage rate of one inch per 30 minutes.

Hall said soil that doesn't meet the minimum requirements is subject to even stricter regulations regarding septic tanks.

That's true, he said, even if the lot is larger than five acres.

Lots larger than 10 acres won't require percolation tests but health department inspections will be mandatory.

The new regulations take effect 30 days after publication in The Sentinel-News. Hall said lots and subdivisions approved prior to the changes would not be affected.

The story could be better. It's a little too institutional and a little less "people" than I prefer. It would be wonderful to talk with developers, builders and an average person planning to buy a home. Their comments would make the story much better.

Wouldn't it also be interesting to see what a homeowner who relies on a septic tank and has constant problems would have to say?

Time was short, as I said. Don't let lack of time, though, become a crutch to justify boring writing.

2. School boards can be just as boring as zoning commissions. In fact, I used to joke that the correct spelling should be "school boreds." As a reporter, find a way to stay awake and somehow determine what's important and what's not.

Let's look at the basics for this story.

Who

On the list are the superintendent and the board members. I left out many others who most likely would have attended the meeting and spoken. You would have to do the same to get to the essence of this story.

What

You might include the fact that no one from the public had anything to say. That's of little importance at this point.

What is important? Several things are – a progress report on construction of an elementary school due to be completed within six months, the need for a 5 percent increase in taxes revealed by a study conducted by the superintendent, a hearing set for Thursday night to give the public a chance to comment, details about the tax and what the cost to the average taxpayer would be if it is approved.

Money is the issue here. It's an important one. If you haven't guessed, something about an increase in taxes must be in the lead.

When
There are several whens in this story. The meeting happened Monday. The school will be finished in six months. The superintendent said a tax increase is needed now. There will be a hearing Friday during which the public will have a chance to comment on the proposed tax.

Where
It's a local story that definitely affects taxpayers who live in the city school district.

Why
The superintendent said existing taxes must be increased if the school system is to pay for the new school. It doesn't answer a major question – how could construction begin if the school system didn't have enough money to cover all costs?

(In actuality, that could never happen. The state would never approve construction unless funding was adequate. This is an exercise, not a real story.)

How
The board has the power to raise taxes and is planning to do so. The public can question the need for the tax, however, and through petitions can place the question on the ballot. Voters could either then approve it or defeat it.

Who cares
Taxpayers certainly do. They will be paying more for the school. Parents and students do, too. A new school can vastly improve the quality of education. There's much at stake here.

What goes in the lead?
Remember, all of this was discussed during a Monday night meeting. The story will appear in Thursday's newspaper. Local radio stations will have the story either Monday night or Tuesday morning.

You need to look for a new angle or emphasize something other than a meeting that will be three days old by the time the story is printed.

How about the public hearing? It's on Friday, the day after the story appears. Why not emphasize that?

You might also want to call a few people to see what they think about the proposal. Some who find out about it might even call you.

Let's pretend that on Tuesday afternoon you received phone calls from three different people, all of whom say they will be at the hearing Friday to protest the new tax and to ask why the money wasn't already in place to build the school.

Your lead might look like this:

> John Q. Citizen wants to know how construction of a school can begin when there isn't enough money available to pay for it.
>
> He plans to be at tomorrow's hearing on a proposed increase in school taxes to voice his questions and opposition.

If no one called, your lead could look like this:

> You'll have a chance tomorrow night at 6 to voice your opinion of a plan to raise taxes to pay for an elementary school already under construction.

Each lead, of course would have to be followed with details about the meeting, how much the tax increase would cost the average taxpayer and the superintendent's reasons for the increase. You would also include what could happen if taxpayers object to the increase.

After the lead is written, add details in logical order. It's really that easy, I believe, to write a story.

Sorting out all of the information and determining what's most important is the hard part.

Include good quotes when you have them. Put them as high up in the story as necessary. In other words, let people tell their own stories when feasible.

3. The Fourth of July Celebration in Campbellsville attracts thousands of people. The annual parade lasts an hour and a half, on average, and the fireworks show is usually watched by at least 10,000 people from many viewing places.

Anything that impacts the celebration would impact many people.

Who

Many could be placed in this category including the board of directors for the celebration, Donna Wise, the Tri-County Car Club, the major donor who withdrew his contribution, city council and the general public.

What

Again, many items could be placed in this category. Among those are the fact the celebration will be July 5 instead of July 4, who the grand marshal will be, the time of the parade, the location for the car show, the shortage of funds for the fireworks, a possible cancellation of the fireworks, a possible cancellation of the entire celebration and an appeal to the public.

I hope you can figure out which one of those is the most important.

When

The change of date for the celebration is a when. The time of the parade is a when. The fact it is June 10 and fireworks must be ordered by June 21 is also significant.

Where

Locations of several events would fit in this category. Overall, it's a Campbellsville festival and the story will appear in a Campbellsville newspaper.

Why

The reason for celebrating on July 5 would fit into this category. So would the reasons for selecting Donna Wise as grand marshal and the reasons for moving the car show. The reasons for possibly canceling the celebration or the fireworks show also fit here.

How

There may be several minor things that would fit here. Hopefully, though, you'll recognize the major item – how the fireworks show can be saved. The answer is money. Money as you will discover is the driving force behind many stories.

Who cares

The thousands of people who attend the celebration should care. Of course, the board cares, sponsors care, the city cares, etc. The celebration is something thousands attend and anything that affects it would affect many people.

Let's summarize. Several things are happening regarding the celebration. The most important, though, has to be the fact that the board doesn't have enough money to pay for fireworks and will cancel the fireworks show if the money is not in hand by June 21.

Also, remember the story will appear in the June 14 newspaper. That's one week before the deadline set by the board to determine if there will be a fireworks show.

Other items such as the date the celebration will be celebrated, time of the parade, location of car show, etc. can all be worked into the story.

The need for money has to come first.

Your lead should be close to this:

> Unless $5,000 can be raised during the next seven days, a fireworks show won't be part of this year's Fourth of July Celebration.

You've got to follow this up with details about the problem. Some quotes from board members and, perhaps, the public would also fit here.

After this issue is fully discussed, the other items can be included. Write about them in order of importance. The reporter will have to make that call.

Remember, the editor might change that order. I would argue, however, with any editor that the financial needs of the celebration must come first. That's especially true, I believe, with a deadline for determining the fate of the fireworks show so close at hand.

4. This is a true story. Names have been changed, and you won't be reading the entire story

.

Who

It's Harold Smith. I don't really see how anyone could not understand that.

What

The story is about Smith becoming the minister at a church that was destroyed by fire and the struggles he faces. It's got to be difficult for anyone to uproot a family and move to another community.

Add to that the tragedy (the words used by many to describe the situation) of a church burning, the need to keep a congregation together and planning for a new church, and anyone should understand the difficulties Smith faces. There are other details that are important, but that's the essence of the story.

When

This could be a bit complicated. Smith is new, so new in fact that he doesn't yet live in Shelbyville. He is moving soon. The church was destroyed five weeks ago. It's not yet certain when the church will be rebuilt.

Where

Hopefully, this is the easy one. The primary focus is the Centenary United Methodist Church in Shelbyville. Smith is from Vine Grove and services are being conducted temporarily at the fire station. Those facts are secondary.

Why

Let's not get confused at this point. The story is not about the church burning. The fact it was arson is not important to this story. The emphasis is on Smith, who he is and why he is facing such a struggle.

How

Smith's ability to deal with the tragedy and become part of the community is the how most people would likely be interested in reading.

Who cares

Members of Smith's congregation certainly would care. I believe most people in the community would also care. After all, a tragedy of this magnitude would greatly affect most small communities.

This is the lead I wrote:

> The Rev. Harold Smith hasn't moved to Shelbyville yet but already he has shared a tragedy.

This lead doesn't answer all of the questions. I readily admit that. This is a feature story, not a news story. Thus, you can entice your reader into the story and provide details later. Personally, I like the lead and believe it works.

If you were reading carefully, you should have noticed that was the way I *wrote* the lead. It is not the way it appeared in print. My editor changed it.

Here's her version:

> The Rev. Harold Smith hasn't moved to Shelbyville yet from Vine Grove, Ky. to assume the ministry at Centenary United Methodist Church, but already he has shared a tragedy.

I was never told the lead was changed. I had to read it in print. To this day I am still upset with that former editor for changing it.

Her version is too long, though it is 29 words, and is a tongue twister on top of that.

If you recall, I recommend no more than 19 words in a lead. Some books may say a lead with 29 words is OK, and in some instances that might be the case. I don't believe it is for this lead.

I'm also going to admit that I never count the number of words in my lead. I include what is needed – no more and no less.

Centenary United Methodist Church is a long name.

So is Campbellsville Board of Education and many other groups, boards, organizations, etc. about which you will write. If you can eliminate their mention from your lead, you will save many words.

I also don't believe it was necessary to include in the lead from where Smith was moving. Who really cares about that? It has its place in the story. But it's much further down.

Details about the tragedy Smith shared had to follow the lead. Add a few quotes from him, and you have a good start to the story.

Include something about his priorities and his plans for the immediate and distant future. Some comments from members of his congregation, especially those who hired him, would follow nicely.

Add some details about his family and his background and the story would practically be written.

Observe, question, think before you write

Pay attention. Ask questions. Sort through all of your notes. Consider what indeed is most important to the majority of your readers. Make your lead as interesting as possible.

Remember, who, what, when, where, why and how are only guidelines. Some elements at times are more important than others. Stress what needs to be stressed.

Never fail to ask, who cares? Understanding how something impacts your readers should always enable you to find the correct lead and to include the necessary details.

Chapter 4
Add some details and you have a story

Now that you've written a few leads, let's look a little more closely at constructing a story. Additional details follow the lead, and they follow in logical order.

As an example, let's talk about a relatively simple story.

The annual Hospice Charity Tea and Auction is Sunday and you're assigned to take photos and write a story. Attending will be folks from all walks of life. Serving tea will be local "celebrities" such as the police chief, judge, mayor, candidates for public office and university president.

First of all, do you know what Hospice is? Who cares?

Well, Hospice provides support to terminally ill patients during their final days. In other words, they help those who are dying and their families at a time when medical care can do no more and death is close.

Hospice impacts many. It's a private, not-for-profit organization that provides care for everyone who needs it regardless of his or her ability to pay. That means fund raising is critical.

How does the tea raise money? For the answer to that question and others you would need to talk to the organizer of the event.

Those who attend must buy a ticket. They are served tea, sandwiches and other treats. Waiting on the attendees are people such as the police chief. They expect tips that will be passed on to Hospice.

The idea of having such "celebrities" wait on everyone is to add a little fun to the event. Any fun at an event that raises money for such a serious cause, of course, has to be tasteful.

Your story also has to be tasteful and should not possibly offend anyone. After all, we are talking about an organization that helps those who are dying. That's a very serious subject.

Money is also raised through a charity auction conducted during the tea. A variety of items each year are donated with all proceeds going to Hospice.

What basic information must go in your lead? The who, what, when, where, why and how, of course. Let's break it down.

Who

In this category are the organizers for the tea, the attendees, the donors and the "celebrities." Each will deserve mention.

What

It's a tea and auction designed to raise money. How much is raised should be in your story.

When

The tea is on a Sunday afternoon. Your story is not promoting it. Instead it will appear after the fact and discuss what happened. The date is secondary information.

Where

The location is the Student Activities Center at Campbellsville University. It needs to be mentioned but is secondary.

Why

The purpose for the tea is to fund Hospice. That's an essential part of the story.

How

Money is raised by the sale of tickets, tips to the "celebrities" and the sale of donated items. This must be in the story.

Who cares

Those who have been served by Hospice probably are at the top of the list. Many may not pay much attention to Hospice unless they find a personal need for themselves or a loved one. Your story needs to show them why they should care. It should attempt to attract everyone's attention.

Sources

The organizers of the tea are obvious sources. So are participants such as the police chief and those willing to slip him a few bucks.

The lead could be something as basic as the following:

> The annual Hospice Charity Tea and Auction Sunday raised $5,600.

While the lead answers most of the basic questions, it's just plain boring and shows no creativity whatsoever. Only those with a great interest and understanding of Hospice would probably read the lead or any of the story. On a ho hum scale of 1 to 10, with 10 being the most boring thing ever written, this lead would have to be at least a 7.

It's certainly possible to be more creative and to entice readers into the story. I began by learning who was in charge of the tea. A phone call to her gave me basic information such as the price of a ticket, who was expected to be serving and items to be auctioned.

I arrived prior to the beginning of the tea armed with my camera, several lenses, a flash, a notebook and several ink pens. Always carry extra film or digital cards. An extra ink pen or two and even an extra notebook are also essential. I've run out of both ink and paper during an interview.

Be prepared.

Because I had done some simple homework, I knew the police chief was among the dignitaries who would be serving tea. I also knew that all dignitaries would be wearing tuxedos.

Part of my plan was to photograph the police chief wearing a tuxedo and serving tea. That's something most people don't see on a regular basis. I took several photographs of him in action.

As I watched the chief serve tea, I noticed something else. People were slipping him money. They were supposed to. The money was the tips for the personal service and all was going to Hospice.

Here's the police chief, I thought, being paid money under the table. I jokingly asked the chief if he routinely accepted bribes. He smiled and said he didn't mind as long as the money went to a good cause.

That quote ended up in the story and also formed the basis of the lead and the second and third paragraphs of the story. Here's what I wrote:

> If you've ever had the urge to slip a few dollars to the police chief under the table, you had your chance Sunday afternoon.
>
> You also could have slipped a few bucks to the mayor, judge or university president. You could have also handed some money to several folks running for office and even a

medical doctor.
   Doing so wouldn't have gotten you in trouble. In fact, it probably would have made you feel good.

On my ho hum scale, where a high score is the kiss of death, this lead has got to rate lower than a 7. I'd like to think it would be as low as a 3. That might be wishful thinking. Regardless of where it would actually fall on that scale, I'm willing to bet the farm (if I owned one) that this lead would attract more readers than the first any day of the week.
   What comes next?
   An explanation of why these people were taking money must. Otherwise everyone probably will be left wondering if all these people are indeed crooks. This is also a perfect place to explain the tea including where and when it was.
   Next comes a little more detail about what was served, what was auctioned, how much tickets cost and how much was raised for Hospice. Many may understand what Hospice is, but a short explanation at this point is a good idea for those who might have no idea.
   I then compared that total to what had been raised in the past. The story winds down with some observations about other servers, their experiences and why they were participating. It concludes with the quote from the police chief about accepting bribes for a good cause.
   That's how the story was put together. I probably spent five minutes gathering information prior to the tea. I was at the tea for about an hour asking a few questions and taking a few photos.
   On Monday, I called the organizer to find out how much money was raised. I then spent about a half hour writing the story.
   Here's the rest of it:

> All of these local "celebrities" were dressed in tuxedos and fetching water and hot tea for about 150 people who attended Sunday's annual Hospice Charity Tea and Auction in the Student Activities Center at Campbellsville University.
>   The money slipped to them was considered as tips and added to the total raised to support Hospice & Palliative Care of Central Kentucky.
>   Those attending were also served sandwiches and other treats. Tickets were $10.
>   Numerous items including an Italian cream cake, pear preserves, framed photographs, original artwork and much

more were auctioned near the end of the annual tea.

Altogether, the event netted about $5,600, according to Carol Sullivan, one of the chairpersons.

The other chairpersons are Mary Lou Rafferty and Dottie Davis.

Friends of Mary Lou (Rafferty) collectively bought the Italian cream cake baked and donated by Leoma White for $1,000.

For the last two years, the amount raised locally has exceeded that raised during a similar tea in Elizabethtown, Sullivan said. She said she was initially concerned that Sunday's turnout might not be as large as hoped.

By the time the tea began, however, there were only a few empty seats.

"I was very pleased," Sullivan said.

Hospice provides support to terminally ill patients during their final days.

Hospice & Palliative Care of Central Kentucky, a Metro United Way agency, annually provides quality end-of-life care and bereavement services to more than 350 patients and their families. A member of the Alliance of Community Hospices, Hospice & Palliative Care of Central Kentucky is a private, not-for-profit healthcare organization dedicated to serving Central Kentuckians regardless of their ability to pay for services.

Community response for Hospice has always been great, Campbellsville University President Dr. Michael V. Carter said as he poured some hot tea Sunday afternoon. Many larger communities, he said, can't match local support.

Dr. Eric Bentley seemed a bit nervous as he wielded a silver teapot. He was smiling, though, as he poured tea for several women who seemed delighted with his attention.

"I'm holding my own," Bentley said.

Campbellsville Police Chief Bill Cassell joked that he didn't mind taking bribes — long as it was for a good cause.

Don't be concerned about taking photographs *and* writing a story. Looking for photographs, I believe, forces a reporter to see details, details that might not readily be apparent otherwise.

The fact I took a photograph of the police chief led me to the quote about accepting bribes. That became my lead.

If you have problems taking photographs and notes at the same time, consider a tape recorder. I never use tape recorders. In fact, I hate tape recorders.

If you have notes, it's easy to consult them when writing the story.

Reporters who rely on tape recorders must listen to the tape, type quickly, rewind and type again or take notes and then write from those. I consider that a major waste of time.

Let's analyze one more story. It's Memorial Day and your assignment is to take photographs and write a story about the annual observation at a monument (the where) that lists the names of those from Taylor County who died during several wars.

I've covered numerous such services. Some were well attended. Some were not. There were always more present when the United States was at war, specifically I'm talking about Desert Storm and the War in Iraq.

One year I wrote about members of the Disabled American Veterans who always conduct the ceremony. They are elderly veterans. All, obviously, are disabled or they wouldn't be members of the group.

They dressed in khaki uniforms and *sat* at attention. They *sat* because they physically were unable to stand for long. I wanted to paint that picture in my lead.

Calling the men elderly, I though, would be disrespectful. After a little thought, I came up with the following lead:

Seasoned soldiers in khaki uniforms sat at attention.

Of the thousands of leads I have written, this remains one of my favorites. There's something about the sound of "seasoned soldiers in khaki uniforms" that I like. I just like it. It's really that simple.

It's a good idea, I might add, to read your leads out loud from time to time. That gives you a feel for what they might sound like to a reader.

This particular Memorial Day celebration was at a time when (as in the when for the lead) the country was not at war.

The primary speaker was the county's oldest living veteran who served time in a German prisoner of war camp during World War II. His comments were especially poignant. I decided to make him the focus (the who) of the lead and much of the story.

His comments, I believe, illustrate the kind of sacrifice (the what) many made for the cause of freedom. They were sacrifices that need to be remembered. That's the reason (the why) there are observances on Memorial Day.

World War II veteran Conrad Claycomb speaks of his treatment by the Germans while he was a prisoner of war. He made his remarks during an annual Memorial Day service in Campbellsville.

    Following his comments and those of another speaker are observations about the service itself. The service consisted of the Pledge of Allegiance, prayer, some short speeches and a 21-gun salute. (That's how the day was observed.)

    Who cares? Veterans and their families certainly do. I would also argue that any American citizen who cares about freedom should too.

    Here's the lead:

> Conrad Claycomb has stared death in the face and lived to tell about it.

    It's simple and to the point. It might be a bit dramatic, but that's OK in my view. Claycomb and others like him risked their lives many times. The statement is accurate. I also hope it rates a low score on the ho hum scale.

The next few paragraphs explain the lead and include some of Claycomb's comments.

> More than a half century ago on a beach thousands of miles away, Claycomb was among the American soldiers who invaded North Africa to liberate it from the Germans during World War II.
>
> "We lost 2,800 men in the first wave," Claycomb said on a rainy Monday afternoon during a Memorial Day service at the Taylor County War Memorial.
>
> Later, during the invasion of Southern France, Claycomb spent days on the beach pinned down by Germans who were "dug in waiting for us. We lost 3,800 in the second wave."
>
> Claycomb was one of seven in his unit who survived but were captured and sent to a prisoner of war camp.
>
> During Monday afternoon's annual service, Claycomb spoke briefly of the nine months he spent as a prisoner.
>
> "We saw the Germans kill their own people," Claycomb said. "They killed those that were too old to care for themselves and belonged in a nursing home. We saw them kill Americans too. If you doubled up your fist at them, you'd be dead.
>
> "The Germans told us that we'd never get out of prison, that it was impossible," Claycomb said. "If you believe in God, nothing is impossible."

At this point, I thought it was necessary to bring the scene back to the Memorial Day service. That was easy to do. Claycomb had concluded his remarks by making reference to the names on the memorial.

> Pausing for a moment, Claycomb stared at the Taylor County War Memorial and the names of those from this community who went off to war and never returned.
>
> "Don't feel sorry for me," Claycomb told the crowd of about 100. "I came home. Those boys over there didn't. Don't feel sorry for me."

Claycomb's comments, used word for word, fit perfectly. After all, he suffered greatly in the cause for freedom. He didn't ask those present to remember him, though, he asked that those who died not be forgotten. I couldn't have made up better quotes that those Claycomb provided.

The story continues with comments from the primary organizer of the service. His comments sum up the reason for gathering on Memorial Day.

> Jack Williams, commander of Chapter 70 of the Disabled American Veterans, spoke of the 130-year history of Memorial Day. He also spoke of the DAV and the many volunteers who assist veterans with transportation to and from hospitals and in many other ways.
> All of these veterans deserve to be remembered, Williams said.
> "We enjoy freedom because they were willing to lay down their lives if necessary," Williams said. "The struggle for liberty may never be over. We must always be willing to do what's necessary. We must also remember what those who came before did for us."

All that's left to do now is conclude the story. That was easy enough. A description of how the service ended accomplished that.

> After a brief prayer during which Williams thanked God for the privilege of living in a free country, the sound of Taps filled the air as those attending stood at attention with their hands on their hearts.
> Members of the DAV color guard raised their rifles and fired a 21-gun salute.
> The service was over. Several walked towards the monument and lovingly, caringly, touched the names of loved ones inscribed in the granite.
> One elderly man turned, saluted the American Flag and then quietly walked away.

I don't know how anyone can be an American, have a pulse and not feel something after reading those few paragraphs.

Resist any urge to alter a quote for emphasis. You are writing reality. Your sources must be real people. Your quotes must reflect what they actually said. All of your stories should be based on facts – this is journalism, not fiction.

Credibility is essential to the journalist. Those who make up stories and otherwise lie to readers hurt all of us. Never, never, never alter reality. The fact reporters for major newspapers and magazines have fabricated stories doesn't justify anyone doing likewise.

In fact, those who have been caught manufacturing sources and quotes, generally have been fired. They should be. I would fire you if I caught you doing likewise.

Observe, listen, feel. That's how you write truthful stories people want to read.

Chapter 5
News affects people

When Fruit of the Loom announced in 1997 that it was closing and more than 4,000 people would be losing their jobs, it was a major story.

There's no way that a plant that large can close in a community the size of Campbellsville without devastating effects. There were many who wondered if the closing would be the end of the community.

People who aren't earning a paycheck quickly change their spending habits. Many businesses wondered if they too would ultimately have to close. There were concerns about real estate values, tax revenue, jobs for young people graduating from high school and college and much, much more.

Families worked at Fruit of the Loom – moms and dads, brothers and sisters, aunts, uncles, cousins.

Many wondered, with due cause, how many people might move away to look for work. They also openly asked if the community, and local leaders, relied for far too long on one factory.

The mayor, who had been in office for decades, wasn't re-elected. Neither was the county judge. People wanted to blame someone – anyone – for the loss of so many jobs. They were obvious targets.

Campbellsville was forever changed because of the plant closing. So were its people.

Some of the initial stories about the plant closing dealt with facts and figures. There were also the usual comments from the mayor, judge and a few other "officials."

The following story was written in early 1997 when significant layoffs at the plant were announced. Sources included a public relations vice president for Fruit of the Loom, the mayor of Campbellsville, the judge/executive for Taylor County, the president of the chamber of commerce and the industrial recruiter for the city and county.

The "official" word from Fruit of the Loom was that the remaining jobs should be secure. This is an excellent example of the need to look at sources other than public relations employees for the company involved.

A complete closing of the plant was announced shortly after assurances that remaining jobs were secure.

Here's the story:

Factory eliminates 1,480 jobs

About half of those employed at Fruit of the Loom's Campbellsville plant will be out of work within 60 days.

The company's employees were told of the loss of 1,480 jobs at the local plant last Thursday morning.

Similar announcements were made at other Fruit of the Loom plants in Kentucky and all over the nation, according to Mark A. Steinkrauss, vice president of corporate relations for the company.

The job reductions will be made in sewing and assembly departments, Steinkrauss said. He said those jobs will be moved "offshore" to locations in Central America, the Caribbean and Mexico.

"We need to stay competitive," Steinkrauss said. "We have to be responsive to our employees, but we also have a responsibility to our shareholders. We also have to protect other jobs."

"It's a sad time for Campbellsville and Taylor County," said Campbellsville Mayor Robert L. Miller. "I feel sorry for those who lost their jobs. This will be a hardship on them. Their quality of life will change."

"This affects everybody," said Taylor County Judge/Executive Fred Waddle.

"This has been stunning and devastating, to say the least," said Marc Whitt, president of the Campbellsville/Taylor County Chamber of Commerce.

The community is going to have to work harder to attract more jobs, Miller said. He said the community is on the right track with a spec building, greater visibility in Frankfort and water and sewer expansions under way.

Whitt said the chamber board will meet this week to discuss what action it can take. A group called Taylor County United will also meet, he said, to begin planning economic strategies that hopefully will ultimately result in new industries and jobs.

A "tough retail environment" coupled with "global changes" brought about by various trade agreements was blamed by Steinkrauss last October for a planned reduction then of 400 jobs.

The company still faces those factors, Steinkrauss said, and had no choice other than to eliminate the jobs.

The planned job reductions last year never completely materialized for a variety of reasons, Steinkrauss said. He said that he believes this time there is no way that the loss of 1,480 jobs can be avoided.

"We are dealing with forces beyond our control," Steinkrauss said. "This is beyond what we can turn around."

Debbie Gray, who works for the Campbellsville Housing Authority and spends about half her time recruiting new industry, said the job loss was inevitable.

"I've been saying for five years that we were going to lose these jobs," Gray said. "No one knew when the loss would come or how many."

Whitt said Taylor County United resulted from the shock waves that followed the announced layoffs last October.

The group has representatives from businesses, local industries, city and county government, education and others, Whitt said. He said the issues have been debated, surveys have been taken and there's a feel for what the area's strengths are as well as its needs.

The announcements last October were a warning, Miller said, but there was little that could be done. It's impossible, he said, to compete with workers in other countries who will sew for 50 cents an hour.

This is not a time to dwell on the past and what should or should not have been done, Whitt said. He said it's a time to sit down together and determine how to best plan the area's future.

Gray said the county has positioned itself to attract industries.

Many prospective industries have looked at the spec building in the city's industrial park, Gray said. She said many prospective industries have also looked at vacant land.

"This is just a long process," Gray said. "Just because a client comes today doesn't mean an announcement will be made in two weeks. Sometimes it can take a couple of years."

The mayor and judge have cooperated fully in the effort to attract new industries, Gray said. She said water and sewer plant expansions will also help.

The fact that many workers will also be available, Gray

said, will also be attractive to prospective employers.

About 150 jobs will be created at the Campbellsville plant in the textile department, specifically in bleaching and dyeing fabric.

Since there were 2,800 jobs at the plant as of June, that will leave about 1,470 jobs at the plant, Steinkrauss said. The sewing department will not be completely eliminated, he said, but the textile department will become the heart of the operation.

Shipping and other support operations will still be needed, Steinkrauss said.

Even with the planned reduction in jobs, Fruit of the Loom will remain the county's largest employer.

At the Jamestown plant, 550 jobs will be eliminated.

Changes in the textile industry have been coming for five years, Steinkrauss said.

There's no way to predict the future, Steinkrauss said, but he believes the jobs remaining at Fruit of the Loom should be reasonably secure.

"Change is not going to stop," Steinkrauss said. "The industry is still evolving."

The loss of jobs is significant to the employees affected and the entire community, Steinkrauss said.

"We know it is very, very substantial. We are working with everybody. We are leaving no bases untouched."

The workers at the Campbellsville plant are "terrific" and "incredible" to work with, Steinkrauss said.

"This is not a reflection of them," he said. "They work hard. It is a reflection of all the global changes that are also affecting other industries."

Fruit of the Loom will be doing all it can to help those employees who lose their jobs, Steinkrauss said.

"It makes my heart ache not only for the people who lost their jobs, but the company and community," Miller said.

Miller said he has been in contact with the Louisville/Jefferson County Economic Development Council which represents 57 industries. Fourteen industries there, he said, are actively hiring.

Some kind of plan could be developed to get those who will lose their jobs to Louisville each day to work, Miller said. He said there has to be a way to get workers there without them being forced to move.

Of those who will be losing their jobs, Miller said, at least 600 are not from Taylor County. He said he has talked with officials in surrounding counties who are also concerned about the loss.

At least 300 of the employees are from Adair County alone. That county was already feeling the economic loss of an OshKosh plant.

"Other counties are going to have to hustle like us," Miller said.

There's no way to make up the loss with one or two new industries, Waddle said. He said it will take a group effort and several new industries as well as expansions of existing industries.

Cox Interior is adding jobs, Miller said. He said he wished the water treatment plant expansion was finished because that could attract many industries.

Taylor County is being noticed and will get new industries, Gray said.

"We have to turn this into an opportunity," she said. "We will survive this."

A look at the basics

Who

The who was Fruit of the Loom, its workers and in a very real sense the entire community.

What

The what was the closing of the plant and all of its implications. Those implications are many including the very future of the area. Without jobs, people can't live. That forces them to move. That affects property values, businesses, schools, everyone in fact.

When

The effects were immediate. They would also reshape the community far into the future.

Where

The entire area was affected. Folks from many counties worked at Fruit of the Loom.

Why

Answering why is a bit more difficult. New trade laws, a failure of officials to see the handwriting on the wall, even greed were all part of it.

How

The consequences of the closing make up the how. What would people do? How would local government respond? What could be done?

Who cares?

Virtually everyone who lived in the area cared. Obviously those who lost jobs or had a family member who was suddenly without work cared more. Anyone who truly cared about the area, though, had a stake in all of this.

Sources

Sources included: Campbellsville Mayor Robert L. Miller; Taylor County Judge/Executive Fred Waddle; Mark A. Steinkrauss, vice president of corporate relations for Fruit of the Loom; Marc Whitt, president of the Campbellsville/Taylor County Chamber of Commerce; and Debbie Gray, the industrial recruiter for Taylor County.

All of these are "official" sources. If time had permitted, employees, business people and members of the general public could have been interviewed.

Etc.

All of the interviews were conducted by telephone. It took about two hours to reach everyone. Many of Steinkrauss's comments came from a press release.

It took about an hour to write the story once all of the information was gathered.

Quite often during the first few days of a major story, facts, figures and "official" comments are about all you will read.

That's understandable. The facts and figures are necessary. Even the "official" comments are important. People need to see the overall picture of what's happening. At some point, though, it is essential that the "human" implications of such a major story be told.

Such was the case of the Fruit of the Loom closing. Thousands of people were affected directly. Thousands more were affected indirectly. It wasn't possible to tell each of their stories. It also wasn't necessary.

The human side of the story

The following story is about Missy Knifley, a divorced mother of one, who suddenly faced a major crisis when her job at Fruit of the Loom was eliminated. There were many Missy Knifleys, of course. Her story, I believe, is representative.

I selected Knifley as the source for my story for several reasons.

A very large percentage of the employees at Fruit of the Loom were women. As was also typical, Knifley began working at Fruit of the Loom almost immediately after high school. As was the case with many other young people, a job at *The Factory*, as Fruit of the Loom was known, was what she always wanted.

She worked a few other places before securing her position, but once she had it, she never wanted another.

Fruit of the Loom was kind to Knifley. She made "good" money and enjoyed a relatively high standard of living. As a single mother, she faced additional challenges as she faced the last few days of employment.

I also knew Knifley. Her daughter had been a member of my wife's Girl Scout troop. Living in a small town, I, of course, knew many others also affected by the plant closing. There were many who likely would have agreed to talk for the story.

Knifley was young, bright and articulate. She was easy to interview and candidly answered all of my questions.

Beginning writers probably should have a list of questions prepared long before a scheduled interview. Experienced reporters may or may not compile a list. I rarely developed questions before an interview.

I always began with general information such as the correct spelling of a name, routine background, etc. A few casual comments, observations about a person's home, etc. also can help break the ice.

It's important to come across as a caring person, genuinely interested in the story you are about to hear. Questions, I believe, generate answers that in turn generate more questions.

The following are some of the questions I asked Knifley:

"When did you go to work for Fruit of the Loom? Did you ever consider any other jobs?

"What kind of work did you do? Did you ever get tired of the work? How well did it pay?

"What kind of life did working there enable you to have?

"Where were you when you heard about the plant closing? What thoughts came to your mind? How did others react?

"There had been many rumors. Were you prepared? How has it changed your life? How will it change your life?"

I spent about an hour and a half with Knifley. That's much longer than I usually spent interviewing someone.

This was a complicated story, and I wanted details.

Normally, I can get most information necessary for a story in 15 minutes, 30 at the most. Rarely did I spend longer than an hour talking to someone unless the subject matter was especially sensitive or complicated.

It's natural that as a reporter you will find many people more interesting than others. Some people also provide more information and better quotes than others. That's just the way it is.

Most news stories can be done by telephone and, in the interest of time, especially if multiple sources are involved, there really is no alternative.

A story such as the one about Missy Knifley has to be done in person. It would be extremely difficult to get this kind of detail and this kind of emotion from a telephone interview.

Plan your time wisely.

This story contains personal details, such as Knifley's monthly house payment, her salary, credit card debt, child support and how much she will receive in unemployment benefits.

These details help paint a picture of how the loss of her job will affect her life and that of her daughter.

They are the kind of details that put a human face on the story. They tell us why we should care.

Knifley readily provided the information. Many might not be so open. As a reporter you must find a way to get people to trust you and open up their lives.

Ask questions in such a way that a yes or no answer isn't possible.

Compel them, in a gentle way, to give you details. If you genuinely care about your subject and his or her story, that will be apparent in your mannerisms and the way you structure your questions.

Again, you can't do all of this over the telephone.

Just a nod of the head once in awhile and eye contact can do much to put your subject at ease.

All of that will result in better answers, quotable quotes and provide a foundation for a much superior story.

Here's the story:

Facing the loss of her job, Missy Knifley keeps busy by weeding a flower bed.

Single mom prepares for loss of job at factory

For the last few weeks, Missy Knifley has been watching her pennies even more closely than normal.

She and her daughter Ashley don't eat out as much.

They no longer rent movies.

They shop for bargains and frequent thrift shops and yard sales.

Putting away every penny possible has become essential to Knifley, 33, a single mother who will be losing her job at Fruit of the Loom along with 1,481 others on Oct. 6.

Knifley's last day of work for the factory will come just three days after her ninth anniversary with the company.

That's provided Knifley's job isn't eliminated earlier. Many units at the factory have already been phased out, she said, and workers sent home permanently.

Those whose jobs have already been eliminated, Knifley said, will be paid as if they had worked through Oct. 6.

After graduating from high school about 15 years ago,

Knifley didn't immediately go to work for Fruit of the Loom. She worked as a clerk for numerous businesses because she enjoyed the one-on-one contact with customers.

Some of those businesses no longer exist.

"I liked talking with people, that was nice," Knifley said. "But it didn't pay the bills. Fruit of the Loom was the best place in Campbellsville to work, for the money and the insurance."

It took Knifley about three years to land a job at Fruit of the Loom sewing T-shirts. Her first day of work was Oct. 3, 1998. She's now a T-shirt examiner.

Going to work at the factory was exciting, Knifley said. She and her husband, from whom she was divorced about five years ago, had just built a home and the extra money came in handy.

"If I had known I was going to get on at Fruit of the Loom, we would have built a bigger house," Knifley said.

Knifley said she has several cousins, an aunt and an uncle who have worked for many years at Fruit of the Loom. Some of them will also be losing their jobs.

"I knew it was going to be hard work," Knifley said. "I don't mind hard work. I like my job. I just wish I could keep it."

As a T-shirt examiner, Knifley must pick up T-shirts, inspect them for any flaws such as holes, runs, or crooked labels, fold them and stack them. She can examine 288 shirts an hour or about one every 15 seconds.

Knifley's pay is based on production. The number of T-shirts she can handle normally earns her about $12 per hour.

Working at Fruit of the Loom, Knifley says, has enabled her as a single mother to be independent. She said she's had no trouble making her house payment and taking vacations to Florida and Las Vegas.

Her house is well landscaped and she has an above-ground swimming pool.

"We were able to eat out and go shopping when we wanted," Knifley said. "We have had a good living."

Knifley has a clear title to her 1988 Nissan Sentra which has 98,000 miles on the odometer. She once also owned a second vehicle, a 1984 Corvette. A few weeks before the job reductions were announced, she had considered buying a new truck.

There were rumors that something might happen at the

factory, Knifley said, and she decided to put off the purchase.

"I'm so glad I didn't buy a new truck."

Knifley said she was holding a T-shirt in her left hand on the morning of Thursday, Aug. 7 when plant manager Chris Reynolds came over the intercom at Fruit of the Loom and asked for everyone's attention.

"We just expected bad news when we heard his voice," Knifley said. "Everybody kind of went silent and had a blank look. My stomach just dropped."

Since then, Knifley said she has watched many become angry over the job losses and lash out at city government, president Bill Clinton and Fruit of the Loom.

"They just want to blame someone, anyone," Knifley said. "Many believe there should be more jobs here. If Lebanon can get them, then why can't we?"

"I'm not angry. I'm just upset that I don't have a job and I am frustrated about that."

Knifley recently had minor surgery on an outpatient basis. It was scheduled on a Saturday so she could work every day possible.

The surgery possibly could have waited, Knifley said, but she went ahead and had it so the medical insurance she has through Fruit of the Loom would cover the cost. She said she likely will have to pay the $302.81 per month her family medical insurance plan will cost after Oct. 6 for a short while.

That's because Knifley must make some follow-up visits to her doctor that she otherwise would have to pay for out of her pocket.

Knifley said she considered going back to school, but medical insurance for her and her daughter are necessities. There's also the question, she said, of what kind of job she could get after continuing her education.

"I'd probably still have to move out of town," Knifley said. "That's something I don't want to do."

The last few weeks have been difficult, Knifley said, pointing out that in addition to losing her job and having surgery, she and her boyfriend of a little more than three years recently broke up.

Knifley said she generally has a positive attitude about most things, but that's been difficult lately.

"I'm trying to stay motivated," Knifley said. "But it's easy to sit in this chair and just stay here. I'm having trouble sleeping and so are many others at the factory.

"I'm trying to make myself confident. I have always been a fighter."

The last day on the job will be tough, Knifley said.

"The days have been going by quickly. It's going to be a sad day. I've made many good friends there. A lot of those people I will probably never see again."

Most employees have stuck together.

"We call each other, we hug each other," Knifley said.

The community has opened up its hearts to Fruit of the Loom employees, Knifley said, and that's appreciated. She said companies such as Comcast which are giving breaks to those losing their jobs are especially appreciated.

Knifley says her doctor in Elizabethtown normally doesn't do surgery on Saturdays, but agreed to when he learned she was losing her job at Fruit of the Loom. Everyone in the office, she said, was helpful and told her of possible job openings.

Knifley said her daughter Ashley, 14, has also been helpful. During one particularly rough week, the teen bought her lunch with her allowance rather than bother Mom.

"She's been a big help," Knifley said.

Education is important, Knifley said, and Ashley recognizes that. She said at one time many didn't think much about education because Fruit of the Loom was there.

In some ways, Knifley may be better prepared to deal with her upcoming job loss than many.

Knifley has a high school diploma and is relatively young. Her house payment is $302 per month. She has no outstanding balance on her credit card and no other monthly payments.

During recent months, Knifley had also saved some money for a truck she had planned to buy. That plus about $3,000 in severance pay she expects to receive will help tide her over while she looks for another job.

She does not receive child support.

Estimates are that Knifley will receive a maximum unemployment benefit of $256 per week.

During the recent job fair, Knifley was recuperating from surgery. Her sister went and picked up information about various jobs and other benefits.

So far, there's been little time to actually spend looking for work, Knifley said. She plans to begin looking in earnest after Oct. 6.

On Knifley's list of job requirements are medical insurance and hours that would allow her to be home each night with her daughter. She's also very concerned about driving very far to work each day since her car does have so many miles on it.

A job in Elizabethtown would be nice, Knifley said, because her sister works there and the two could go together.

"I just hope and pray that something will become available. I'm very scared of the unknown and what's going to happen."

A look at the basics
Who

The story is about Missy Knifley, of course, but in a larger sense it is about every person who worked at Fruit of the Loom.

It's also about anyone who has ever lost a job or had a family member or friend who lost one.

What

The story is about how one person, representative of the larger whole, has faced a tragic situation. It's about the human condition. It's a story of what happens to people.

When

The closing for Fruit of the Loom is an unfolding news event. It's also a timeless story because many have lost jobs in the past and many undoubtedly will lose jobs in the future. It's about dealing with adversity.

Where

It is Taylor County. It is also the region. It is also any place that has ever faced a major plant closing.

Why

There is more than one "why" in this story. Why did the plant close?

The story doesn't detail that so much because others already had. It deals more with why Knifley depended so much on the job and why her life was changing.

How

Knifley's story is representative of many and shows how a plant closing affects people. Through the experiences of one person, the story conveys how the entire community is affected.

Who cares

Knifley certainly does. So do her co-workers, friends and family. Anyone living in the community also cares. A community cannot lose so many jobs without devastating effects. As unemployment increases there's less money for residents to spend. That means other businesses will also suffer.

Other jobs also could be on the line. Real estate values could drop as many sell and move elsewhere to work.

The story about Missy Knifley is actually the kind that almost anyone, anywhere, at any time could find interesting. It's about what can happen to people. It's real and details the human condition.

Sources

The only source for this story was Missy Knifley. After all, it is her story.

Etc.

The Fruit of the Loom closing was reported in many stories. Others detailed efforts to recruit new industries. The community has recovered and arguably is now better off than ever. Diversified industry means a single plant closing can no longer result in such devastation.

All of that, however, was told in many other stories.

The story about Missy Knifley doesn't tell all in the lead and is not written in inverted pyramid style. It is written more as a feature story though I would classify it as news. Weekly and semi-weekly newspapers often have to take feature approaches to news stories.

Why?

Simple.

Anyone who really cares probably already knows all of the facts by the time the story appears in print. Reporters for anything other than a daily newspaper must strive to tell the story in a different way or provide fresh facts.

If time permits, tell more than the "official" story. Let the people speak. Show us why we should care.

News stories can be about many subjects. That's especially true in a relatively small community.

Some newspapers are actually so small that there may only be one reporter who also doubles as the editor.

It's also true that reporters for even large papers at times may cover a wide variety of topics. Those topics could include education, politics, taxes, employment, zoning regulations, business, leash laws, farming and much, much more.

Such variety, I believe, help makes the job interesting.

It's impossible to discuss in any detail every possible subject. Before leaving news, let's look at one more topic.

This time the story is about farming.

Since many of my relatives have farmed, primarily to supplement their incomes, and I raised tobacco to finance my college education, farmers have a special place in my heart. Farmers remain important to many communities and if you work in an area where farming is still important, odds are that at some point you will be down on the farm.

The next story we will look at is about a father and son who have made farming an art as well as a science.

The story won a first-place award from the Kentucky Press Association in the business/agribusiness category.

Harvest of Plenty

Noble Howard's corn yield among tops in state, nation

On gently rolling land kissed by Pitman Creek, Noble Howard last year raised more corn per acre than anyone else in the state and virtually everyone else in the nation.

And he did it without turning even one shovel full of dirt.

Howard has been raising corn since 1973 and has never tilled his land. Over the years, he has turned no-till farming into a science which he says pays off with high yields while protecting the soil.

Last year's yield of 243.46 bushels of corn per acre placed Howard first in the Class A No-Till Non-Irrigated division of the 1994 National Corn Growers Association National Corn Yield Contest in Kentucky.

Howard's harvest placed third in the nation.

"This is the best I've ever done," Howard said.

The story about Noble Howard was written in winter. There was no corn in the field. So I had Howard hold some ears of corn in front of the bin where the crop is stored until it is sold.

There were 2,383 entries from 46 states in the contest. The average yield for all the entrants was 192 bushels per acre.

Howard farms with son Marion who began raising corn in 1979.

Last year, Marion managed to raise an average of 215 bushels per acre which was good enough for fifth place in the state. The Howards jointly farm 630 acres, 500 of which is cropland, off Moss Road.

Marion usually raises about 100 acres of corn, and Noble usually raises about 110.

Though Marion last year succumbed to his father's mastery in raising corn, he holds the record for the highest yield so far recorded on their farm. In 1982, he produced 249 bushels per acre, the highest in the state.

Neither of the Howards were members of the National Corn Growers Association in 1982, so Marion's yield that year wasn't entered in national competition.

Both believe it likely would have been the top yield in the nation.

Raising good quality corn in large quantities requires a

combination of factors, according to Noble.

"This doesn't happen by accident," Noble said of the yields he's constantly been able to produce. "You have got to plant it right. The only thing that really is uncontrollable is the weather. You have to depend on the good Lord for rain."

It takes good land, Noble said, plus perfect weather and proper fertility, which is aided with fertilizer applied before planting. Insect and weed control are also essential, he said, and accomplished with chemicals.

Fertilizer is applied a short time before planting. Without fertilizer, Noble said, he "couldn't produce 50 bushels to the acre."

A six-row corn planter was modified by the Howards to inject the insecticide Furidan directly into the row and under the soil when the seeds are planted, Noble said. Marion said the tractor that pulls the planter is equipped with a sprayer carrying herbicides.

The herbicides are pumped to six sprayers located directly over each row on the planter.

"We can make one pass over the field and put down the weed control, insect control and plant our corn," Marion said.

"Then we watch it grow," Noble said.

Marion said application of chemicals is controlled from the cab of the tractor. And the micro-injectors are so accurate, he said, that one quart of Furidan can be applied per acre.

The fact the chemicals are used in sealed containers and never touched by hand, Noble said, makes their use much safer. He said injecting Furidan directly into the ground and then covering it with soil also prevents any danger to birds or other animals.

The process, Noble said, is approved by the U.S. Environmental Protection Agency while some other once commonly used methods of applying chemicals aren't.

The Howards also raise about 300 acres of soybeans and 80 acres of wheat.

When corn is combined, a cover crop is immediately planted. It's actually planted from the rear of the combine so an additional trip over the field isn't needed.

The Howards farm their land without additional help.

"We don't hire any help at all," Marion said. "We try to be as efficient as we can."

Each of the Howards has three silos and can store 45,000 bushels of corn between them.

They often sell corn on a contract basis with delivery

perhaps months in advance. Selling when the market is high, Noble said, more than makes up for storage costs.

The Howards use a computer to monitor daily and weekly weather patterns which might affect their crops. They also use it to keep up with grain markets.

"Farming isn't anything like it used to be," Noble said.

Noble will be honored for his high yields later this month in a ceremony in Nashville.

This is his slow time of year, so he'll be there for the ceremony. In a few weeks, though, it will be time to prepare the soil for yet another year of corn production.

A look at the basics
Who
The story is about Noble Howard and his son Marion.

What
The subject is how successful the Howards are at raising corn and the fact their yield was so large that they placed first in the No-Till Non-Irrigated division of the 1994 National Corn Growers Association National Corn Yield Contest in Kentucky and third in a national contest.

It also emphasizes that this feat was accomplished by lovingly nurturing the land.

When
The award the story hinges on was to be presented a few weeks after the story was published.

When also refers to the constant attention the Howards pay to their corn.

Where
The crop was raised in Taylor County where the Howards live. That made it a local story. There were two awards – one that was statewide and one that was nationwide.

Why
The Howards received their award because of their success.

How

The Howards' success was possible through their hard work, attention to detail and use of technology and the latest farming innovations.

Who cares

While this is not an earth-shaking story, it is not every day that two local residents do something better than anyone else in the state or most in the nation. It is significant from that standpoint.

The story matters to the Howards as well as those who know them. I believe it also matters to the community because it demonstrates what someone who works hard and intelligently can accomplish.

Sources

The only sources for this story were the Howards.

I might add some comments here about the lead.

"On gently rolling land kissed by Pitman Creek, Noble Howard last year raised more corn per acre than anyone else in the state and virtually everyone else in the nation."

What does the word "kissed" add to the sentence?

Does it impart a sense of closeness to the land, a love of the land?

I hope so. That was the intent. There's also something about the sound of that word in the lead that I like.

The lead actually also contains this sentence: "And he did it without turning even one shovel full of dirt."

What kind of lead is this? Is it a direct lead, the kind you would find in most stories written in inverted pyramid style?

(Direct means it takes you directly to the essence of the story.)

Or is it a delayed lead, a lead that has a sense of mystery about it and takes awhile to get to the main point?

It's a delayed lead, the kind most feature stories usually have. This story is news, in my opinion, with elements of a feature.

The essence of the story is actually revealed in the next few sentences:

"Howard has been raising corn since 1973 and has never tilled his land. Over the years, he has turned no-till farming into a science which he says pays off with high yields while protecting the soil.

"Last year's yield of 243.46 bushels of corn per acre placed Howard first in the Class A No-Till Non-Irrigated division of the 1994

National Corn Growers Association National Corn Yield Contest in Kentucky.

"Howard's harvest placed third in the nation."

News stories, indeed, can touch on many subjects. And while most may be written in the inverted pyramid style, that is not a necessity.

Chapter 6

Features – everyone has a story to tell

It was a cold and stormy night.

Lightning flashed in the distance, briefly illuminating the barren landscape. The wind howled like something from an early Stephen King novel.

OK. I'll stop. That's probably not the best way to begin a chapter on writing feature stories. Though the three sentences are nothing to brag about, for some odd reason I enjoyed writing them.

Don't ask why. I really don't know.

You should enjoy writing a feature story. In fact, most reporters enjoy feature stories immensely. Writing a feature provides a break from news, which at times can be hectic, frustrating and controversial.

Most reporters also tend to write feature stories about subjects that interest them.

Features detail the interesting things people do

In general, features are more detailed than news stories. They are usually written more as short stories with one major exception – they are always true.

Forget about the inverted pyramid when writing a feature. Get creative. Experiment with leads. Throw many of the rules about writing news out the window.

Don't forget, though, that your lead must be eye-catching. It must grab the reader and encourage him to stay awhile. Your story must also focus on people doing interesting things.

I can't imagine doing an interview for a feature story over the telephone. Such an interview has to be done in person. You have to take in the entire scene. Look at photos on desks, what's hanging on the walls, the books a person keeps close by.

Such observation can lead to questions that, in turn, can give you some great quotes or take you down a road you had no idea even existed. Details are essential for a feature story.

Don't tell us, for example, about an old car with red paint.

Paint pictures with words

First of all, the term old can mean many different things to many different people. What kind of cars are considered compacts? Are you even certain that the car you're describing really is a compact?

And red, please, I'm a car nut. No manufacturer was ever content to merely paint a car red.

They use colors such as torch red, candyapple red, Cardinal red, Redfire clearcoat, crimson red, Colorado red, etc., etc.

"She drove a candyapple red 1966 Mustang" means much more to me than a reference to an old, red compact car. The details paint a visual image, a detailed image for those familiar with the look of a classic Mustang.

Without those details, the reader only has a rough outline or sketch of what you are trying to convey.

Fill in that outline.

Consider the following:

"The car began to shake, slightly at first, just a gentle back and forth motion that I could feel in my seat. As we accelerated from 55 to something approaching 100 mph, everything in the car that wasn't firmly bolted down also began to dance.

"Even my knees were jiggling as we turned onto a narrow one-lane road built at a time when vehicles were pulled, not driven, by horsepower.

"My teeth began to chatter as our speed topped 150 mph. I began to wonder if I would survive my first ride in a Ford GT, a modern-day, street-legal race car only those with more than $125,000 to spare could ever think about possessing."

Is there a visual image there? I think so.

I also believe it's better than the following: "I went for a ride in a new Ford GT. We went really fast, and I was a bit scared. The car is expensive and only a few people will ever own one."

Paint pictures with words.

There are as many feature ideas as people, maybe more

Ideas for feature stories are everywhere. Everyone, I believe, has a story to tell. A good reporter knows that and can find those stories.

Look for folks with interesting hobbies or unusual ways of occupying their spare time. Keep your eyes open for those who prefer green concrete to grass for a yard. Tell the story of the man who lives next door and spent two years in a POW camp in Germany during World War II.

How about the person who collects walking sticks, match box covers from all over the world, antique toys or soda pop bottles?

Almost everyone has a collection, some of them unique.

How about the story of the dog who slept on his master's grave?

My wife once did a story about the death of a man who was widely known for attending every funeral in his hometown. Who attended his funeral? Who would continue his tradition of paying respect to his neighbors?

Simple stories can be best

A feature can be simple, as simple as Girl Scouts visiting a nursing home.

I spent a couple of hours one afternoon watching, listening and taking notes and photos as a group of shy young girls visited a few elderly women. It took me about an hour to write the following story:

The power of love

Local Girl Scouts share time, feelings with elderly nursing home residents

Nervously, Lauren Abell and Ella Knifley approached Vivian Pierce.

Pierce, who is in her 80s, was seated at a table in the dining room of Medco Nursing Home where she had been working on a quilt.

The three were silent for a moment.

With a little encouragement from one of their Brownie Girl Scout leaders, Lauren and Ella introduced themselves and explained that they were at the nursing home to "adopt" Pierce.

A smile crossed Pierce's face and she hugged each of the girls.

The three began talking about quilts, doll clothes, and the like. Then they trotted down the hall to look at the room Pierce calls home.

Meanwhile, 16 other first-, second- and third-graders were getting to know the grandparents they have "adopted."

In the lobby of the nursing home, Leslie Blevins and Amber Priddy were engaged in a lively discussion with Viva Gilpin, a retired school teacher who is also in her 80s. Gilpin was telling the girls about students she had many years ago. And the girls were telling her about their fellow classmates and teachers.

Other nursing home residents were showing photos of their real grandchildren, who live far away, to some of the other Brownies.

By this time, Lauren and Ella had returned from looking at Pierce's room. They paused to look at an aquarium and the many fish behind the glass walls.

All three appeared to be having the time of their lives.

It was soon time to leave. And many of the girls gave their "new grandparents" a hug before leaving as well as a promise to return soon.

"The girls have all been very excited about adopting grandparents," said Barbara Brown, leader of the Brownie Troop 1450.

"All of them had visited nursing homes and they said there were lonely people there," Brown said. "I was surprised that girls their age were so aware of such things."

The troop meets every other week with a visit to the nursing home as part of its activities. But Brown said the girls also make it a point to either visit or contact their "grandparent" each week.

The program is part of a national effort by Girl Scouts. And the 18 girls will receive a patch for their efforts. The program will officially end after Christmas. But Brown said many of the girls will continue their visits long after that.

"It's made a lasting impression on many of the girls," Brown said.

The nine residents at Medco who have been "adopted" are all very excited about the program, according to Lisa Lawson, activities director. She said more residents could use such visitors.

Residents relate well to children and pets, Lawson said. She added that many don't have visitors often and may not see their own grandchildren as often as they would like. The visits, she said, become especially meaningful.

"It excites them to know they are going to have visitors," Lawson said.

The visits have been very touching, Brown said.

"You can tell in their eyes," Brown said, "that they

were pleased that little girls could have so much love for them."

A look at the basics
Who
This story is about different generations getting to know each other. It is told through these little girls and the residents of the nursing home.

What
The story details how much different generations have in common and how important it is for all of us to become a family.

When
The time is now, an afternoon at a local nursing home. In a sense, though, the story is timeless.

Where
It is right here, at home, in a place many people might pass every day and think little about.

Why
The story shows how much a few caring people can mean to someone who is lonely and has much to share. It also shows how, through a few simple acts and a little time, all of us can become family.

Sources
This story was done in person. Sources were the Girl Scouts, their Scout leader and the residents of the nursing home. It's a simple story told through the participants.

Etc.
There simply was no way to do this story other than in person. It relies greatly on details and observations. Also, at a small newspaper you will be both the reporter and the photographer.

I probably spent about an hour at the nursing home gathering information and taking photos. I spent about an hour writing the story.

Let your sources tell their own stories when appropriate. Observe, take notes and write what you saw and heard.

The quotes and observations from the participants are, in my opinion, what makes this story.

At least some of my peers must have agreed. It won a first-place award for feature writing from the Kentucky Press Association.

Though feature stories generally are not written in inverted pyramid style, basic information must still be included. Features must also be relevant, that is they must matter to the reader on some level.

Writers often write about subjects that interest them

It should not come as a surprise that many writers prefer certain types of stories or subjects.

During my time as a reporter and editor, I did my share of stories about subjects I love. That includes gardening and Mustangs.

The next story we will discuss is about a customized Mustang. It graced the covers of many national magazines.

The story was justified even if I had not been a great fan of Mustangs. After all, how many people in your community have been featured in national publications?

Not many, I would say.

The fact I was interested in cars and knew the subject of this story was to my advantage. I knew the subject and didn't have to do much research.

Let's look at the story:

Red heat
Custom Mustang graces pages of national magazines

When Gary Patterson was putting together his custom Mustang, he often spent hours researching and debating many planned modifications.

He didn't have to think twice about the color though.

The car was going to be red, the brightest red Patterson could find.

"Red is the color magazines like," said Patterson, who is a quality control manager for Ingersoll-Rand in Campbellsville.

Perhaps it's the color that initially attracts onlookers at

Gary Patterson cleans his Mustang at a national show in Charlotte, N.C. sponsored by the Mustang Club of America. I combined business with pleasure and was there with my Mustang.

the national meets Patterson attends on an average of once a month. But it's modifications such as a 1970 351 Windsor engine with fuel injection and a 200-horsepower nitrous system, a sound system any audiophile would envy and countless other options Henry Ford's engineers never dreamed of that make them look twice.

Whatever the reason, Patterson's custom Mustang, which is known as Red Heat, attracted the attention of the editor of Muscle Mustangs & Fast Fords during the Ford Motorsport Nationals almost a year ago in Pennsylvania.

"It was a big national meet and all of the magazine guys were there," Patterson said. "The editor saw me and said he wanted to shoot it for his magazine."

After several appointments were rescheduled for a variety of reasons, Patterson in late March finally trailered his Mustang to the studio of Steve Coonan in Connecticut.

Coonan, Patterson said, is one of the leading automotive photographers in the country and has photographed album covers including one for ZZ Tops' Eliminator.

For almost 10 hours, Coonan photographed Patterson's Mustang from every conceivable angle, paying particular attention to the "goodies" readers of the magazine would most likely be interested in seeing.

Patterson returned home and soon received a telephone call from John Hunkins, a writer for Muscle Mustangs & Fast Fords. Hunkins asked him numerous questions about the Mustang, the modifications and how a native of Greensburg ended up building such a car.

Then Patterson began waiting for the issue of the magazine in which his car was to be featured.

He didn't have to wait long.

In July, Patterson received a copy of the September issue of Muscle Mustangs & Fast Fords. On the cover – the full cover – was his car. A small photo appears on the index page which shows him "in the fenderwells" cleaning his car for the photo session while his nephew Jeremy Coffey looks on.

Red Heat, as it turns out, is the featured car in the September issue of the national magazine. Another five pages and nine photos are devoted to it, all in color.

Patterson was pleased.

One of his goals since beginning the Mustang in 1990 was to be featured on the cover of a national magazine.

"My objective was a cover," Patterson said. "You have to set a goal and go for it. And you have to go somewhere to be seen."

Red Heat has been to several national shows sponsored by the Mustang Club of America and taken first places in categories for modified Mustangs. It's also been featured in other national magazines including the May 1992 issue of Mustangs & Fords, the December 1992 issue of Mustang Monthly and a special publication known as Car Craft 5.0 Performance.

During one national meet, Patterson met Steve Saleen who has made a name for himself by modifying, with Ford's permission, new Mustangs. He said he's also on a first-name basis with many of those whose Mustangs are regularly featured in national magazines.

Patterson's car was also one of eight in the country to compete in Car Craft Real Street Eliminators in St. Louis in late June. The car was tested on the road and the drag strip and evaluated along with the seven others.

Red Heat was also photographed and will be featured in the November issue of Car Craft magazine.

Specifications for the car are lengthy. The engine sports a .030-inch overbore, balanced crank, ported 1970 DOOE heads with 1.94/1.60-inch valves, TRW 9.5:1 pistons,

Edelbrock Performer RPM cam and intake, 7-quart Canton oil pan, Melling high-volume oil pump and Holley Pro-Jection 4 fuel injection.

With the nitrous system, it produces an estimated 600 horsepower.

Red Heat has a custom fuel and exhaust system. The suspension was also modified to handle the extra power.

The car features an interior he salvaged from another Mustang he wrecked in 1990 on the way to Carl Casper's Custom Auto Show in Louisville.

Red Heat also has a roll cage for safety. Patterson said a roll cage in the Mustang he wrecked probably saved his life.

The interior features an Alpine 7903 CD tuner, a pair of quad-channel Yamaha amps, a Coustic XM-3 crossover and an Audio Control equalizer. The system powers a pair of Boston Acoustic 8-inch subwoofers, a pair of Polk Audio front speakers and a pair of Alpine 6 1/2 – inch speakers, all housed in a custom enclosure.

There's also a security system with remote door entry.

Red Heat began its life as a 1980 Mustang with a four-cylinder engine and an automatic transmission. It has 1990 LX taillights, a 1986 TG front bumper and side moldings, SVO sail panels, 1990 convertible rearview mirrors and a variety of other parts from several years. The door handles have been shaved and the antenna frenched. There's also a cowl induction hood.

Patterson readily admits he gets some kidding from his co-workers, especially when he drives the car to work. Many, he said, don't believe he actually drives a car that has been featured in national magazines and won national awards.

Patterson began building model cars at age 7 and built his first "real" car at age 15.

His father was a parts manager for Ford and helped impart his love for the Blue Oval.

As much as he enjoys the attention Red Heat gets, Patterson said the real joy is in driving it. He's 38 years old and also gets his share of ribbing for building and driving what many consider a teenager's car.

Patterson is building another custom Mustang for Coffey. The car will feature a Thunderbird front end, and he said it should be "nicer" than Red Heat.

A 1965 Mustang fastback is also "aging" in the back yard of his home near Greensburg. He plans to someday rebuild and modify it.

"I'm going to build it the way (Carroll) Shelby should have," Patterson said.

As for Red Heat, "I'll sell it to the right guy with the right money."

A look at the basics
Who

This particular story is, of course, about a Mustang, but it's about much more than that. It's a story about a man who set out to build a car worthy of national recognition. He achieved that goal. I'm willing to bet that few in your community can brag that their car has been featured in several national magazines.

What

The story details how hard work and persistence can make the dream of building something, in this case a car, that attracts the attention of national magazines, a reality.

When

The time is now. Like any good feature, though, it is a story that could be published virtually anytime without losing any of its appeal.

Where

It is right here, at home, and shows that local people can do impressive things such as being featured in national magazines and becoming known in some circles on a national level. Even a reader who isn't car crazy should be able to appreciate the hard work something such as this requires.

Why

Does the story completely explain why someone would go to so much trouble and expense to build a car? Probably not. Someone who loves cars, though, needs no such explanation.

Who cares

Those who know me should not be surprised that I've written stories about car people, especially those who have Mustangs.

The story, hopefully, is interesting even to those who don't share my passion for Mustangs or other classic cars but can appreciate the hard work and skill it takes to do what Patterson did. Car fanatics without a doubt will care more about this story than those who think of a car as nothing more than transportation.

Hopefully, though, those who know Patterson would also find the story interesting. And many in the community do know him because of his occupation. The fact that he and his car also appeared in several national magazines should interest many.

You don't have to like cars to recognize that it takes something out of the ordinary to have such great success.

Sources

Gary Patterson was the sole source for this story though I did read the magazine articles about his car.

Etc.

The story obviously had to be done in person. How else could you possibly describe the car and why it has attracted so much attention?

Detail was important. Other car fanciers definitely wanted to know what made Patterson's ride unique.

It helps if you are interested in the subject.

If you're not, it probably would be a good idea to seek out an expert before the interview and get a quick lesson in what to look for and what questions to ask. Reading a magazine or two might be a good idea, if time permits.

No one can be an expert on everything. If you don't know something, ask. Sooner or later all of us will be asked to do a story about something that doesn't interest us in the least.

It's also impossible to explain something to a reader if you don't understand it yourself.

Over the years I have been amazed at how interested I have become in subjects I initially thought would bore me.

Approach all of your stories with an open mind.

Sharp readers will notice that Patterson's car is red, "the brightest red he could find."

The story, however, does not state the specific name of the paint he actually used. It should have.

It's OK at times to write about stories that interest you. Just don't over do it. Two stories about cars over 20 years shouldn't be too much.

One a week definitely would raise some eyebrows.

In a small community, you will also be writing about people you know. That's just part of being a reporter.

The trick is to maintain your objectivity. Someone once told me that a good reporter has no friends. I hope that's not the case.

Just be careful when you write about a person you know well or a topic that greatly interests you. Be certain that no one or no thing has gotten special consideration.

You must care to be a good writer

Let's look at another feature story. An acquaintance told me about Francisco Garcia, a Mexican immigrant, who was making his home in Taylor County.

Garcia was very much aware that the number of Mexican migrant workers was increasing. It was his desire to do something to help those moving to the area make an easier transition.

A religious man, Garcia found inspiration in an abandoned church he passed almost daily on his way to and from work.

His idea was a simple one. He wanted to buy the church, rebuild it and preach the Lord's word in Spanish.

Talking to Garcia inspired me. His story was one I wanted to tell. I truly believed that his story would inspire others. It was a story, I also believed, that might help him fulfill his dream if readers shared his vision and offered to help.

The fact that I cared about Garcia and his dream didn't bother me one bit. Some might think that reveals a lack of objectivity on my part. I disagree.

An ethics book I have used on many occasions talks about the need to be fair, balanced and disinterested.

Reporters of course should be fair and their reporting should be balanced. There's nothing about the story I did I consider to be unfair. There's also nothing about it that I consider to be out of balance.

Had there been neighbors surrounding the building who opposed its use as a church, I would have printed that.

That wasn't the case. Neighbors welcomed the fact the building would no longer be abandoned. There simply was nothing controversial about Garcia's dream.

During the interview, Garcia did make a comment about migrant workers who didn't know the Lord.

The comment was controversial and likely would have been considered offensive by many. It wasn't included in the story.

Why?

The comment served no purpose.

It added nothing to the story. Including it would have required comments to "balance" Garcia's abrasive opinion of those who do not believe in God.

In short, I believe my story was fair and balanced.

Does it reflect disinterest on my part? I'll let you decide that.

To be disinterested means to not care. Stating that a good reporter must be disinterested might sound good in principle. But, how can anyone write anything meaningful if they don't care?

I believe it's impossible.

A writer can be somewhat detached. A writer can seek a diversity of opinions. A writer can seek "truth" wherever it might be found.

But how can a writer write stories that people care about if he or she doesn't care?

I believe that caring makes you a better writer. I believe it allows you to see the human side of issues.

Just remember your obligation to "truth" and the need to present all sides of an issue.

Here's the story about Francisco Garcia:

Rebuilding God's house

Once abandoned, church will offer sermons in English and Spanish

For several years, Francisco Garcia paid little attention to the decaying brick building that he passed several times each week on his way to and from work.

The lot adjoining the building was overgrown with weeds and brush. A steeple which made it clear that the building was once a house of worship was intact, but weathered from years of neglect.

After accepting the Lord four years ago, Garcia said he started seeing God's presence in places he had often looked but never really seen.

One day last year, Garcia was passing the rotting church and was compelled to take a closer look. He discovered that it was once the Tallow Creek Methodist Church and, though neglected, could still serve the Lord.

"I used to go by here all the time," Garcia said. "I never had it in my heart that I was going to buy it and preach in it. God has messages for all men if they will listen. He told me I was going to buy this building and make my church here."

Garcia inquired about the building and discovered that the owner, George McDonald, was willing to sell. The asking price was $7,000.

A bank loan for $4,500 helped complete the deal as winter was ending, Garcia said, but he had to come up with the balance in two months.

As the owner of a small farm in the Dry Creek area, Garcia supplements what he can earn from his own crops by working for other farmers. Raising the balance of the money for the church, he said, and coming up with cash for improvements wasn't easy.

The Lord was watching, Garcia said, and trees on his farm which he didn't believe would be large enough to cut for timber were ready early this spring.

Garcia, who lost three fingers on his right hand in an accident a few years ago, bought a chain saw. He and his 15-year-old son Juan cut the timber which fetched $6,000.

Not long after purchasing the church, Garcia was approached by Robert Boston who "felt led by the Lord to go up there."

"The church was just a shell," Boston said. "I discovered who owned it and we worked out a deal."

"He wanted to lease it," Garcia said. "I told him that the title is in my name but doesn't belong to me. It is God's building. I told him he was free to use it.

Garcia said Boston has been "a blessing."

Boston is helping with the renovation. And after the church is ready, both men will use it to spread God's word.

Garcia will be conducting services in Spanish and Boston will be conducting them in English. Both believe that if they will preach, many will come.

There are hundreds of Spanish-speaking people in the area, Garcia said. He said many live here year-round, others come and go with the crops.

The number of migrant workers is increasing, Garcia said, but there are few churches that offer services in Spanish. He said he believes people will come from as far away as Somerset for his sermons.

Those who speak little or no English, Garcia said, can't get much out of a service that's not in their native language. Instead of feeling God's joy, he said, those who don't understand what's being said become frustrated.

"This should mean much to them, " Garcia said. "To come to church and listen to God's word should make you feel happy."

The church will become an extended family for many from Mexico who come here a few months out of the year to work, Garcia said. He said most people in the area and the farmers the migrant workers are employed by have been really good, but there are spiritual needs to also meet.

Boston said the church will no longer be Methodist. It will be non-denominational with people of all faiths and backgrounds welcome.

Garcia and Boston have decided to call their house of worship the Tallow Creek Community Church. Both hope it will appeal to many who are all part of the community of God.

Several people who live in the Tallow Creek area and haven't attended church for a while, Boston said, have told him they will attend once the building is ready.

Garcia and Boston both work during the week. That means renovations are made in their spare time and on Saturdays.

Sunday is a time for worship, not work, Garcia said.

Some extra hands, church pews and building materials are what's needed most, Garcia said. He emphasized that he is not begging for donations and will build the church on his own if necessary.

Help is also needed with an air conditioning and heating system, Boston said. Volunteers willing to help replace the floor which was eaten away by termites are also needed.

Boston may be reached at 789-1364 and Garcia may be reached at 606-787-6359.

Garcia believes the church will easily hold 120 worshipers.

It would please him if there's quickly standing room only and an addition is necessary.

Someday, Garcia would like to see the church grounds expand. A swimming pool and other recreational facilities would be nice, he said, and serve not only migrant workers but others in the community.

For now, though, Garcia and Boston are concentrating on the basics so the church can open as soon as possible.

"I would liked to have had services last Sunday," Garcia said.

A look at the basics
Who
Francisco Garcia was the primary subject and source.

What
The story is about Garcia's efforts to rebuild an abandoned church and preach to migrant workers in their native Spanish.

When
Though the story did not have to be published immediately, time was a factor. Garcia needed help with his dream. The sooner the story was printed, the sooner that help might be forthcoming.

Where
There are a couple of wheres in the story. It was within Taylor County, specifically in the Tallow Creek area. That means nothing to someone who doesn't live in the area. "Natives" know exactly where the church is.

Another where could be what Garcia hopes the church will become, a place where people of all faiths can worship and a center that the entire community can use.

Why
Garcia identifies with migrant workers. A Mexican himself, he knows what it's like to be far away from home. The story, hopefully, explains his inspiration and belief that God wanted him to restore the church.

How
Hard work, determination and vision answer that question. It's also answered by an understanding bank willing to make a loan and Garcia's strong faith in God.

Sources

Garcia was the primary source for the story. Robert Boston was a secondary source. If time had permitted, neighbors in the area could have been interviewed as could have been migrant workers who might attend the church. Another minister or two also could have been asked about the role the church might play.

Would those additional sources have added significantly to the story? Probably not. Nevertheless, it probably would have been a good idea to talk with some others.

If you work for a community newspaper, it can be difficult to find much time to devote to a feature story. You do the best you can with the time you can find. That's just the way it is.

Etc.

Garcia did receive assistance with his dream after the story was published. He was grateful for the story and called to say so. That's not the kind of feedback you will get from many of the stories you write.

Writing the story made me feel good.

The fact Garcia's dream was well received by others did too.

Not long after leaving the employ of the Central Kentucky News-Journal I passed by Garcia's church. It appeared to be abandoned again. I don't know what happened.

There's probably a story there waiting to be written.

Let's look at one more feature story.

This story was somewhat unusual. It featured a doctor who normally practices on humans operating on a horse to remove cataracts.

The Gift of Sight

Surgery partially restores horse's vision

The patient's legs were bound to the operating table with rope.

His midsection was secured with large nylon bands and a series of chains. On his head was a special halter, which was also tied to the table.

Pumping through his system was an anesthetic known as G.G. which was enough to keep all 1,300 pounds of him unconscious while doctors worked to restore at least part of his sight.

The patient was Surprise, a Tennessee walking horse

gelding with cataracts who is owned by Dr. W.R. Mann.

Prior to his surgery Saturday afternoon at Cox Animal Clinic, the horse was completely blind. He had only one good eye when Mann obtained him about a year ago. And Mann noticed after riding the horse a few times that vision in the other eye was rapidly "going."

Though he's not a vision expert, Mann suspected that cataracts were responsible for Surprise's loss of sight. He said he also suspected that there were other problems such as glaucoma.

Cataracts, glaucoma and other vision problems develop in animals as they get older just as they do in humans, according to veterinarian Dr. Ben Cox.

He said most animals, however, don't receive treatment for such vision problems because of the cost.

Mann said he couldn't stand the thought of Surprise, who is 14 years old, being blind. So he asked Cox and Dr. Thomas G. Abell, an ophthalmologist, if they would try to restore his vision.

Though Abell normally treats only humans and specializes in such techniques as laser surgery, Mann said he immediately agreed to do the operation.

Since neither Abell nor Taylor County Hospital has an operating room large enough to handle a horse, Cox Animal Clinic was chosen as the site of the operation. And Cox accepted the task of anesthetizing Surprise and assisting Abell.

Upon his arrival at the clinic, Surprise was given a mixture of drugs to help him relax.

His legs were wrapped so he wouldn't hurt himself while being strapped to the operating table.

The table has a hydraulic lift so animals as heavy as a horse can be strapped to it in an upright position and lowered.

Abell brought with him a variety of surgical supplies, though the equipment he had on hand wasn't designed for someone with four legs and weighing 1,300 pounds.

"He may not be the best looking patient you've ever had, but he's the biggest," Mann told Abell as he arrived.

A quick examination of the horse's eyes by Abell revealed cataracts as well as glaucoma and possibly some other problems as well. But he said he believed surgery would at least partially restore the horse's sight.

Cox and his assistants led the animal inside the special building constructed for equine and bovine surgery.

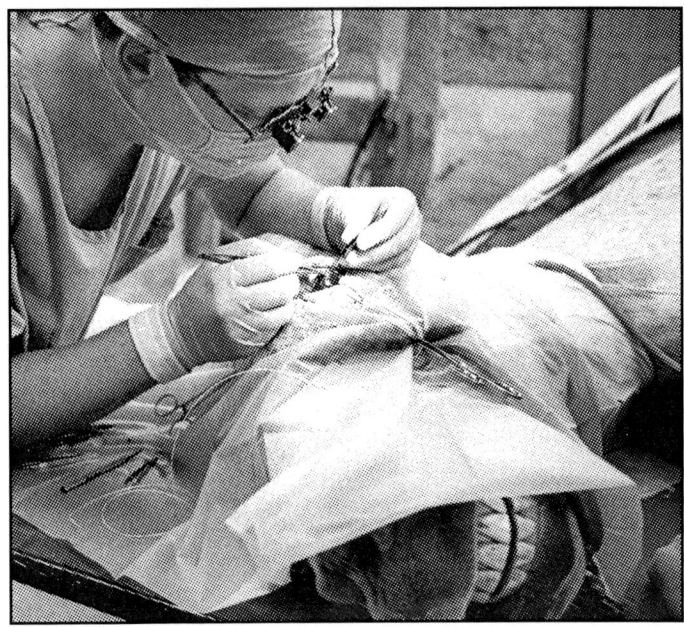

Ophthalmologist Thomas G. Abell removes a cataract from Surprise, a Tennessee walking horse who was going blind. The horse regained partial sight after the surgery.

Surprise was secured to the operating table which was in an upright position. Cox then gave the horse an injection of a form of pentobarbital that immediately "put him under."

The operating table was lowered to a horizontal position and an IV of G.G. was started. After Cox checked the horse's vital signs, Abell began the operation.

Abell had hoped to use a device that can produce temperatures of 80 degrees below zero to remove the cataracts. But the machine malfunctioned, and he had to resort to other surgical techniques.

"This is the kind of medicine that was practiced 50 years ago on humans," Abell said.

As Abell operated, an occasional fly buzzed about. Because the room itself could not be made sterile, he used sterilized cloths around the horse's eye and wore his usual surgical gown and mask.

A special pair of glasses also helped him better see the horse's eye.

Antibiotics were constantly applied topically to lessen

the chances of infection.

Within about 30 minutes, Abell had removed the cataract from the horse's left eye and had stitched it with absorbable silk.

That will eliminate the need to remove any stitches later.

To work on the other eye, Surprise had to be turned over.

"That's probably going to be the hardest part of the operation," Abell said.

Cox and his assistants Danny Givens and Chris Newton grabbed Surprise by the legs and pulled him towards them. They then rolled the horse over on his back and finally had him laying on his other side.

A towel was placed under the horse's head to cushion the eye that was just operated on.

Abell began examining the right eye and quickly discovered massive scar tissue.

The scar tissue was so bad, Cox said, that even if the cataract were removed, the horse would be unable to see.

The decision was made to leave the right eye alone.

The IV of G.G. was removed. Altogether, about six pints of the anesthetic were used to keep the horse under for the 45 minutes or so the procedure took.

The operating table and Surprise were moved to the open door of the building. Bales of hay had been scattered outside for the horse to rest while he regained consciousness.

The straps were removed and Cox and his assistants slid Surprise off the table and onto the hay. Slowly, the horse began to awaken.

A patch and bandage were applied to the horse's eye. And Cox, Mann and Abell watched closely as the medication wore off enough that the horse could go home.

Abell said the horse would require medication and a great deal of care for a few days.

The bandages were removed Sunday morning. And Cox said Surprise reacted to a hand in front of his eye and apparently had regained some vision.

"Dr. Mann has a soft spot in his heart for his horses," Cox said.

Mann was appreciative of Abell's and Cox's efforts and was pleased that Surprise will see again.

A look at the basics
Who
The story is about Surprise and the love Dr. W.R. Mann had for him. It's also about an ophthalmologist who cared enough about Mann to perform the surgery.

What
Specifically, of course, the story is about an operation to restore Surprise's eye sight. It's unusual because such operations are rarely performed on horses and certainly not by an ophthalmologist.

When
The story was timely and published a few days after the surgery. Many, I believe, would still find it interesting years later.
That's typical of a feature story.

Where
All of the participants are local.
The operation was performed at a local veterinary clinic.

Why
A man's love for his horse is the reason for the operation.

How
Most of the focus of the story is how cataracts are removed from a horse. Indeed, as the story points out, just putting a horse under to work on his eyes is quite a job.

Who cares
I would like to think that anyone with a heart would be touched by this story.
Patients of Dr. Abell certainly got a glimpse of the human side of the man who routinely performs laser surgery and modern-day miracles.
Animal lovers also should have been pleased that so many people would go to so much trouble and expense for a 14-year-old horse.

Sources

Dr. Mann, Dr. Abell and Dr. Cox were the primary sources. Observation also was key to this story.

Etc.

It obviously required cooperation of all involved for this story to become a reality. Many surgeons don't like outsiders observing them work. The priority also was the horse, not a reporter taking notes and photographs.

Detail is important to this story. What kind of drugs and what quantity are needed to anesthetize a horse? Where do you find an operating room large enough for a horse, and once you do, how do you secure him to the table?

The first few sentences of the lead don't make it clear that the patient is a horse. It describes the use of robes and chains to bind the patient to the table. One might think something criminal is happening.

The reality of the situation is made clear soon enough, though. The fact photos of the operation also appeared with the story also eliminated any mystery.

Quotes were used to emphasize the central theme of the story – the love of an animal and how all of us can assist others.

At least one person close to Dr. Abell was concerned that many might read the story and come away with a negative opinion of his ability. The fear was that some might wonder why a noted ophthalmologist would do surgery on an animal.

I believe Dr. Abell's patients who read the story were impressed by his actions. The story, in my view, portrayed him as a man who cared about a fellow physician and was willing to help his beloved horse.

Those reading the story certainly didn't want it to end after the operation was over.

Could Surprise see?

That's a question that had to be answered. The answer took time. Thus, the story had to wait until a determination of the surgery's outcome could be made.

Luckily that only took a few days. The results were also positive. Surprise did have some vision, thanks to those who cared.

Chapter 7
Sports

Many people are great sports fans. Some, in fact, ignore all other sections of the newspaper and head directly to the pages that tell them who won, who lost and all of those other statistics that teams keep.

I am not a sports fan.

It's ironic, I suppose, that my first job with a real newspaper was as a summer sports writer. I spent evening after evening watching kids play, or attempt to play, baseball and softball.

I collected statistics though I barely knew what an RBI was.

I wrote about who was going to "clinch" the title and those who were "sliding" into last place. To my surprise, I discovered I enjoyed and was actually pretty good at photographing sports.

One of the first awards I ever won from the Kentucky Press Association, in fact, was for a photo of a little boy sliding into home with another player leaning over him with the ball in hand. I just never could get into writing a play-by-play story about a game.

At some point I discovered that sports wouldn't be possible without people. And I realized that I could write stories about people.

That realization made all of the difference in the world.

Good sports writing, I believe, is more than a summary of a game or event. A good story talks about the people, their struggles, their dreams, their achievements. That kind of stuff even interests me.

Look beyond the statistics. Look for details as you would when writing a feature story.

Several years ago a fellow reporter at The Sentinel-News, Jack Brammer, and I were assigned to cover the Shelby County Rockets' trip to the Sweet Sixteen. He wrote the stories. I took the photos.

(The Kentucky High School Boys State Championship Basketball Tournament is called the Sweet Sixteen. Why? After district and regional play, 16 teams go to the championship.)

The Rockets and the two of us went all the way to the finals in Louisville's Freedom Hall. When the Rockets won the championship, Jack knew he had to have something different for his lead.

After all, major media from all over the state were at the game. The story appeared in many newspapers. It wouldn't appear in our newspaper for a couple of days and by then anyone who cared would know who won.

Jack had to have some detail no one else had.

Jack did have one ace in the hole. He knew Coach Tom Creamer and knew him well. After all, he had covered the Rockets for months, not just one game. That gave him access and the background necessary to come up with something different.

After talking with the winning coach after the game and asking a few select questions, Jack had what he was looking for, a detail the major media didn't care about. It was a detail that showed the human side of the coach who now had a state championship to call his own.

It's been too many years for me to recall the exact lead and a copy of the newspaper was not readily available for reference.

The lead, though, was similar to this:

"After winning his first state championship, all Coach Tom Creamer wanted was a cup of his wife's homemade vegetable soup."

Even a non-sports fan can appreciate some good food. I might also point out that this story, one of the biggest sports stories ever for The Sentinel-News, used a feature approach. The lead didn't even specifically mention basketball or include stats of any kind.

It emphasized people.

During my years in the newspaper business, I wrote more features, news, editorials and columns than sports.

As I have already said, I spent my first summer in the business writing about Little League and similar sports. I also wrote many features, some news and took photos of all kinds.

At The Sentinel-News, in addition to writing news, I covered women's basketball as both a writer and photographer. My stories were not full of statistics. They had some play-by-play because most people expect that. But they also emphasized people.

I came to know and respect the women's coach, Charlotte Chowning. The team played hard but hopes of a championship were crushed during one crucial game.

I'll never forget the headline I wrote for that story: "There's always tomorrow for dreams to come true."

There's some editorializing in that headline. I admit it. In sports, though, it's possible to interject an opinion on occasion. I remember dropping by the local fire station for some information about fire runs and seeing that headline on a bulletin board.

It's great to see your work clipped and posted for all to see.

The following was written for The Sentinel-News:

Debbie Marshall's 'new family' allows her to play Rocket basketball

She loves to play basketball and she wants to go to college. With a little luck and a lot of hard work, she may get to do both.

But for Debbie Marshall it may not have been possible had it not been for the friendship of Jimmy and Rita Edwards.

Last summer Debbie's parents divorced. She wanted to stay in Shelby County and play basketball since she and her coaches feel she may obtain a scholarship. The Edwards offered to become guardians for Debbie and provide her a home here.

It is a relationship which has worked out well. "I really like it," Debbie said. "They try to help me the best way they can."

The Edwards have a four-year-old daughter Andrea whom Debbie thinks a lot of. On occasions she baby-sits but she says she loved every minute of it.

Jimmy Edwards acts as a coach for Debbie and she says she appreciates his advice.

"He's always trying to make me a better player," she said. "He comes to the games and tells me what I did wrong and the whole team. I also play softball on the Pacers and he's the coach for that."

Debbie's parents, Lewis and Nettie, come to games whenever possible. But, while growing up she was influenced most by her brother William.

There's a little bit of Tom Boy in every girl and Debbie says William helped bring out the part of her. He is largely responsible for her playing basketball.

She has two sisters, Patty and Geraldine.

Basketball is a lot of fun for Debbie, but she admits she likes to win. According to Coach Charlotte Chowning, she is "the" ball handler for the team.

"We rely on her for points and for speed," Chowning said. "She can shoot with her left hand and with her right and she has good jumping power."

College is a major goal of Debbie's and she is considering the University of Louisville and Georgetown. She said she may major in journalism.

Her hobbies include macramé, jogging, horseback riding and camping.

Debbie attributes her success in basketball to God. "He gave me the talent to play," she said.

One thing that disappoints Debbie most about playing for Shelby County is poor attendance at the girls' games. She says it is especially frustrating when a visiting team has more fans.

But there are at least three fans Debbie can count on being at the games – Jimmy, Rita, and Andrea Edwards.

"They make me feel like part of the family," she said. "I really enjoy being around them."

A look at the basics
Who
This is very much a people story about Debbie Marshall, a senior basketball player.

What
The story is about Marshall's dreams and how others are helping her make them a reality.

When
Marshall is a senior. The story talks briefly about how she got where she is and where she hopes to go. It's about the present but also focuses on the future.

Where
It's a local story, pure and simple.

Why
Friends, hard work and God are part of why Marshall is who she is.

How

Friends who care, coaches who care and a young woman who care are how Marshall will succeed. The story details that caring.

Who cares

The how for this story explains much of who cares. It's also a story with which most sports fans and parents should readily identify. Hopefully, it's also one that might inspire other young people.

Sources

Marshall, Coach Charlotte Chowning and Jimmy and Rita Edwards were all interviewed.

Etc.

This story is not about a ball game or any other specific sporting event. It is about the life of one athlete and the people who support her. Sports is much more than statistics and numbers. It's people. Any good writer should be able to do stories about people even if sports is central to the theme.

Most of my duties at the Central Kentucky News-Journal revolved around news and features. I did cover some sports if there was a particularly important game or championship coming up. I also wrote a sports story that won a first-place award from the Kentucky Press Association.

That story focused on an individual. It was also about a sport that doesn't get as much attention as basketball, baseball or football. That made it of special interest to me. I like traveling the road least traveled.

Jason Keltner races to win on go cart tracks across the country

Wearing a black jump suit with blue racing stripes, Jason Keltner takes a quick look at the oval dirt track only a few feet away. He then slips on his gloves and helmet.

Nodding to his father Terry, Jason slides into the go cart which hugs the rocky soil.

With one quick crank from Terry, the 5-horsepower engine comes to life.

Jason makes a couple of quick adjustments to the carburetor and then rams the gas pedal to the floor.

Dust flies as Jason, who is 13, makes his way onto the short track.

Within seconds the Briggs and Stratton engine is turning between 5,300 and 5,900 rpms. The operating temperature is a blistering 280 degrees Fahrenheit. And Jason is circling the track at speeds approaching 40 miles per hour.

That's not bad for an engine virtually identical to those that power garden tillers.

Jason has the track to himself during this practice run. But during races on Sunday afternoon, there could easily be a dozen or more other go carts each fighting for the lead position.

Since he began racing almost a year and a half ago, Jason has eaten little of anyone else's dust. He's won the majority of the races he's competed in, an average of one each weekend.

Jason has won so many races, in fact, that his nickname is "The Jet."

Last December, Jason took his go cart to Daytona, Fla. and raced against some of the best drivers his age in the country.

One hundred drivers attempted to qualify for the Daytona World Speedway Championship during the last week of December. Only the top 25 raced in the finals for the title.

Jason managed to qualify in the 19th position.

During the 15 laps of the race, which is "just down the road" from the famous Daytona stock car track, he passed 18 go carts to take the lead. When the race was over, he took the checked flag and the title.

"It was the first time a rookie ever won it," Terry says of his son's victory. "And it was the first time anyone ever won it starting that far back."

Jason only smiles as Terry talks about his son's racing career.

"He doesn't say much," Terry explains. "He prefers to be behind the wheel."

Jason's first race was in October of 1993 at Mannsville Cart Raceway. He placed second.

"We knew then that he had potential," Terry said.

Jason Keltner races around the track during a practice run. His go cart can hit speeds of 65 miles per hour and more.

After numerous victories at Mannsville, Jason and his go cart sought out regional competition. He competed in and won the Midwest Dirt Classic in Columbus, Ohio. He also won the 100-lap Hillbilly 100 in Somerset last year.

"That's the biggest race in Kentucky for the Junior Sportsman class," Terry says.

Terry is a veteran stock car racer. Initially, he discouraged Jason from racing.

But after retiring from racing himself, Terry decided that perhaps Jason could carry on the family tradition.

"It's something he wants to do and he's good at it," Terry says. "He'd drive that go cart around the track all day if somebody didn't stop him."

Jason's go cart is painted blue, the same color as the stock car Terry once raced. He also uses the same number, "0", which his father once used.

The go carts burn ethanol and can reach speeds of 65 miles per hour or greater.

Go cart racing can be dangerous, Terry says.

Recently at Somerset, there were three accidents with drivers taken to the hospital. All of the accidents happened moments before Jason raced.

"I was on edge," Terry said, "But there's danger in most things anyone can do. Jason played football and tore his ligaments. He's a careful driver."

Though the engines are stock, they are usually hand-assembled and blueprinted to produce the maximum power possible.

Jason's engine was built by Junior Gowen, a noted engine builder in Memphis, Tenn.

A well-tuned engine can cost $600 to $700, Terry says.

Gowen is often at national competitions and assists Jason with mechanical work.

The frame of the go cart is made of chrome molly tubing. The body is fiberglass.

Competition go carts have disc brakes and chain drives. Rear tires are usually 7 inches wide while front tires are 5 inches.

The tires are about 34 inches in circumference.

The cart itself, without engine, costs between $1,800 and $1,900.

A good engine and cart, however, are just the starting points for racing.

Knowing how to use them properly is fundamental to victory.

Jason and Terry do all of the setups for the go cart.

"We've probably got 40 to 50 sets of tires and different gear ratios," Terry said.

Track conditions can vary greatly depending on temperature, moisture, and other factors.

One of the keys to winning is selecting the right tires for the track conditions. Much of the engine's power can be lost if the tires don't have the right amount of bite.

Ask Jason if he understands how to select the proper tires for varying track conditions and he'll respond with a simple, "yes."

Jason in fact understands the science of racing so well

that he helps set up go carts for other drivers.

In his class, go carts plus rider must weigh 275 pounds. Each go cart is weighed at the end of a race. Those which don't weigh 275 pounds are disqualified.

Since Jason weighs only 75 pounds and the cart itself weighs 125 pounds, additional weight has to be added.

Distributing it properly is also another key to winning.

Terry said in national races competitors who suspect that an engine has been modified can protest.

By posting a required fee, Terry said, the driver protesting can have the suspect engine torn down for inspection.

Nationals are operated under strict standards, Terry said.

Some races offer cash to winners. Others offer prizes and trophies.

Jason said there's not been a lot of money in winning so far. But he's accumulated a lot of hardware for display.

Numerous sponsors help offset the cost of racing, Terry said. He said he'd like to obtain enough sponsors so that Jason could run the entire national circuit.

There are point standings for that, Terry says, just like in stock car racing.

And the top points driver at the end of the year does benefit financially.

Terry says Jason's win at Daytona has gained the attention of many sponsors. He's hopeful it will propel him to bigger and better things.

Jason plans to compete in as many national races as possible this summer. And he plans to be back at Daytona in December to defend his title.

What's his secret to winning?

"I don't know," Jason says. "I just like to race."

A look at the basics
Who

Jason Keltner is the primary subject of the story, though his father is mentioned and quoted extensively. Jason preferred to drive his go cart instead of talking.

What

The story is about a young man who has raced go carts all over the country. It is about determination, hard work and a dream.

When
The time is now. The story, however, does mention past accomplishments including a major one just a few months prior. It does not hinge on one particular victory or accomplishment. That means it could be published almost anytime without losing any of its value.

Where
It's a local story, the kind local newspapers should print. But the story also takes the reader to other places briefly, even Daytona, Fla., for one of the largest go cart races in the country.

Why
The story details that part of the competitive spirit within most of us. It's a spirit most can relate to, even those who are not rabid sports fans. It looks at why someone would devote so much time to pursuing a dream.

How
Hard work, practice, skill and even some luck can result in victory. The story details how Jason got started, how he made it to the big time and what it takes to stay there. He later went on to successfully race mini-trucks.

Who cares
Most sports fans, especially those into NASCAR, would likely care and relate to the story. I believe any father and son could also relate as could anyone with a dream.

Many in the community also could relate to a young man who at a tender age races in national competitions and generates much exposure for his hometown.

The Chamber of Commerce had to love him.

Sources
The primary source should have been Jason Keltner. Unfortunately, he just didn't want to say much.

That made his father Terry the main source. The story does end with a quote from Jason, a quote that perhaps sums up the story.

Look for quotes that do that. I might add that I never use a tape recorder. I almost hate the things.

You have to play the tape back to hear what was said. It's much easier to edit and search through your notes.

There is a trick, though, to taking good notes which making good observations and taking photos.

Etc.

I spent a half hour or so talking with Jason and his father at their home. Jason, as I already said, talked very little. Getting just a few words out of him was difficult.

Photos were needed to accompany the story. Since the Keltners didn't have a track at their home, arrangements had to be made for an action photo.

I didn't want a posed photo of Jason with his go cart.

It would have been great to have followed him on the race circuit. My boss wouldn't spring for a trip to Daytona, so I did the next best thing.

Jason practiced on a regular basis at a track in a nearby county. So on a nice afternoon shortly after the interview, I followed the Keltners to the dirt oval and watched as they unloaded the cart and prepared for action.

That observation allowed me to include the details that I believe add much to the story. You'll notice that the story is written in present tense. I described what I saw including the dust and the speed.

The result, in my opinion, was a much better story and photos.

The story and photos, in fact, occupied a full page in the Central Kentucky News-Journal. I was pleased and so were the Keltners.

Working for a small newspaper, I might add, provides the opportunity to devote a large amount of space to something such as this story and photos. On a large daily newspaper, the story likely would have been much shorter if it had been used at all.

Don't dismiss smaller newspapers. I prefer them. And I believe that in general they do a much better job of covering the people who make up the community.

One last bit of advice – sports is much more than statistics or basketball and football. People do all kinds of things in the name of sports. Some might even consider restoring and displaying cars as a sport.

Focus on people. If you do that you can't go wrong.

Chapter 8
Obituaries – a matter of life and death

The inevitable conclusion to life is death.

Some people's deaths, for many reasons, are more news worthy than others.

Some lives end tragically and unexpectedly. Such stories must be approached with compassion and sensitivity.

Obituaries can be among the most important and best-read stories in a newspaper. Many often are printed on the front page because of the prominence of the individual or the tragic nature of an individual's death.

The majority of obituaries are supplied by funeral homes. They usually contain basic information such as who, what, when, where, why and how. For most people, that is usually sufficient. For some, it is not.

If we apply the standards for determining news value to obituaries, some do become more important than others. Don't get me wrong, that's not saying that one life is worth more or less than another.

Some people, either through who they are or who they become, are especially noteworthy. The death of the president of the United States, for example, is going to get more ink and better play than John Citizen.

A local citizen who worked tirelessly to raise money for cancer research and every other cause imaginable and dies from cancer probably deserves a front-page story. So do individuals who have devoted themselves to public service and worked hard all of their lives to improve the community.

Infamous people such as Charles Manson will also be featured prominently in all media when they die.

That's just the way it is.

A terrible disaster or a tragedy might also push someone's obituary from inside the newspaper to the front page. People who die at age 80 in their sleep don't attract much attention.

Those, however, who die young as a result of a shooting rampage or some other tragedy find themselves in the public eye.

That's also just the way it is.

An obituary is a person's life story. It deserves to be written with care and dignity.

Most people will have their name printed in a newspaper three times – when they are born, when they get married and when they die. That's worth remembering.

Suicide is a reality of our world. It's one of those topics that is often debated and handled by many media in many different ways.

Should the fact someone committed suicide be reported?

You or your newspaper will have to make the final call. But, in some instances, I believe it is necessary. If the president of the United States, for example, killed himself should the American public know that?

I think so.

If the mayor of Campbellsville commits suicide, should the residents of Campbellsville know that? Most likely.

If an armed man walks into a local store full of customers and kills himself, should the press report that? Definitely.

Most media have a policy of some sort regarding suicides. Most newspapers I am familiar with consider the prominence of the person involved, the details surrounding the death and whether or not it took place in a public place. Suicides committed in private and not directly involving the public generally were not written about.

A word of advice – be certain it was a suicide before saying so. I recall a death several years ago in Campbellsville. Everyone *knew* the man use a gun to kill himself. The coroner, however, determined that the man was cleaning his gun and it accidentally discharged, fatally wounding him.

Most people believed the coroner covered up the suicide. His official word, though, is what mattered.

Let's look at a story about a local woman who had championed many causes including the battle against cancer. She was well known. Her photo appeared often in the newspaper in relation to yet another project she was heading.

After a long struggle, she lost her battle against cancer.

I knew the woman well. A simple obituary somewhere inside the newspaper simply wasn't enough.

Writing the story wasn't easy. I knew the woman and greatly respected her. While writing the story was difficult from an emotional standpoint, the fact I knew her made it easy to determine what had to be included. It also made it easy to find those who knew her and would share their thoughts about her death.

Friends, 'family' remember Rita Goldstein

If a program in any way benefited people, Rita Goldstein most likely was actively involved.

That's what friends of Goldstein, who died Monday, had to say about her.

"She was an active person, concerned about the community in every way," said Wilma Gaddie, a close friend and fellow member of the Campbellsville Business and Professional Women's Club.

Though Goldstein suffered from cancer for more than 20 years and sometimes was quite ill, she never complained, Gaddie said.

"She thought about everybody but herself."

Gaddie said Goldstein moved here more than 20 years ago with her father, the late Samuel Goldstein, one of the founders of Parker-Kalon.

Goldstein, 67, was born in the Bronx, N.Y. on June 24, 1930. She graduated from Hunter College and was elected to Phi Beta Kappa.

After teaching high school for a few years in New York, Goldstein went to work for Parker-Kalon and moved with the company several times before coming to Campbellsville. She was an expert with computers and retired from the local plant.

Gaddie said the community quickly embraced Goldstein.

Goldstein also embraced the community, becoming involved in numerous clubs and programs. She was president of the local chapter of the American Cancer Society at the time of her death, a position she had held for many years.

Goldstein for years, also spearheaded an arthritis drive for the BPW club.

"She was able to get money none of the rest of us could," Gaddie said. "She had no close family. She made the community her family."

Goldstein was so successful with arthritis drives that the club won several awards for generating so much money, said Sylvia Morris, current BPW president.

"Rita is BPW as far as I'm concerned," Morris said. "She's been the backbone of the club, held every office and won every award."

Morris said Goldstein was the "glue" which held the BPW club together.

"She was always very giving," Morris said. "She was a very committed person. She was community minded and worked hard. She kept all of us driven to do our best. The community is going to miss her."

Goldstein was a supporter of women's causes long before there was such a movement, Morris said.

"She kept us aware of women's causes and worked for equal opportunities. She lived and breathed to do all she could for the community. She motivated us and made us realize that we can all make a difference."

The BPW club last year paid special tribute to Goldstein and her many accomplishments.

"Campbellsville did become a home for her in every meaning of the word—the community became her family."

Father Jack Caldwell agreed.

Caldwell said he first met Goldstein about seven years ago during a Catholic church gathering.

"I had heard a lot about her, about all of the community work she had done," Caldwell said.

Caldwell said he soon discovered just how much the community meant to Goldstein and how dedicated she was to helping people. Raised as a Jew, Goldstein joined the Catholic church, he said, and soon was busy also doing the Lord's work.

Goldstein served on the parish council, helped plan Bible school, worked with various committees, was in charge of fund-raisers, read scriptures in church, was a member of the Legion of Mary and did much, much more, Caldwell said.

One fund-raiser that Goldstein seemed particularly glad to be involved with raised money to send youngsters to camp, Caldwell said.

Last year, Goldstein received a Stewardship Appreciation Award from Our Lady of Perpetual Help. The award, Caldwell said, is one way the church was able to express its appreciation to her.

Goldstein was ill for years, Caldwell said, but never complained.

"She seemed to have that extra strength," Caldwell

said. "She promised the Lord she would do his work. There seemed to be no end to it."

During the last few weeks, Caldwell said, when Goldstein knew death was imminent, she still didn't complain.

"She was still smiling and trying to help other people."

Goldstein was also a Hospice volunteer.

Arrangements were handled by Parrott & Ramsey Funeral Home.

Terry Dabney, owner and operator of the funeral home, said he had worked with Goldstein on many projects including the acquisition of hospital beds and other such equipment for those who were ill. His wife Judy also worked with Goldstein on various programs through the American Cancer Society.

"Though she had health problems of her own," Terry Dabney said, "she was always more concerned about others' problems. It was impossible to tell her no when she asked for something to help someone."

Goldstein died Monday at 9:05 a.m. in a Greensburg nursing home.

Visitation will be after 4 p.m. today at Our Lady of Perpetual Help Catholic Church. Prayer vigil will be at 7 tonight at the church.

The funeral is tomorrow at 11 a.m. at the church with Caldwell officiating. Burial will be in the church cemetery.

Survivors include three cousins: Dr. Rosalie Fisher of Livingston, N.J.; Mariam Hevey of LaPlata, Md.; and Dr. Jerry Treen, provost at Harvard University in Cambridge, Mass. She is also survived by a special friend, Sherry Koopersmith of Northboro, Mass.

A look at the basics
Who
The story is about Rita Goldstein, an extraordinary person.

What
It's about her death. It's about the community's loss. It's about how much of a difference one person can indeed make even if they are in pain and dying.

When

The story is the summation of a life. It is now, but it's also the past and, perhaps, even a glimpse of how the community will never be the same without Goldstein.

Where

It's a local story, of course, something local media should focus on and be better at writing than anyone else.

Why

The story details the cause of Goldstein's death but it also celebrates her life.

How

Hopefully, the story tells us how we can live better lives by following Goldstein's example.

Who cares

Anyone who knew Rita Goldstein cared. Many who didn't know her also should have cared because odds are that her volunteer work impacted them in some way.

Sources

The funeral home was an obvious source. The most telling parts of the story, however, come from those who knew and loved Rita Goldstein.

It took several phone calls and a few hours to reach everyone. It was time well spent, in my opinion.

Etc.

Lives such as Rita Goldstein's deserve to be celebrated and remembered. If you're assigned to write an obituary, don't consider it a chore, consider it an honor.

Over the years, I encountered more suicides than I care to remember. One took place on the campus of Campbellsville College. That fact alone was deemed enough to justify printing the story.

Many people desperately wanted to know why Judi Stewart decided to take her life and why she chose to do so in an office where she once worked and apparently had been happy. There were no ready answers.

(Stewart killed herself in September after leaving the employ of the college in July.)

Former secretary to president takes her life at college

Those at Campbellsville College who knew and worked with Judi Stewart are still trying to understand what led her to fatally shoot herself in a back room of the president's office last Thursday morning.

Stewart, 42, had worked for the college about 13 years when she left her job as executive secretary for President Dr. Kenneth W. Winters in late July. She left to accept a position as data base manager with the Association of Independent Kentucky Colleges and Universities in Danville and assistant to vice president Tom Prather.

Though she was no longer an employee of Campbellsville College, Stewart was on campus on a regular basis. She apparently still had access to the president's office because she was helping train a new secretary.

Stewart was seen by an administrator at the college about 7 a.m. About 45 minutes later, her body was found by Winters inside a workroom of his office.

Taylor County Coroner Terry Dabney said no autopsy was performed. The investigation, he said, led to "no doubt in anyone's minds" that Stewart had died as the result of a single, self-inflicted gunshot wound. Letters left by her and other evidence, he said, led to that conclusion.

The death was investigated by Dabney, Campbellsville Assistant Police Chief Carl Dobson and Kentucky State Police Detective Dennis Benningfield.

Notes written by Stewart for the police chief, the coroner, relatives, and Winters were found in the office, Benningfield told the Lexington Herald-Leader.

"They were just mainly telling everybody she's sorry for the trouble and things like that," Benningfield said.

Benningfield said the notes indicated that Stewart chose

to end her life in the president's office because she felt most comfortable there.

Marc Whitt, director of public relations and marketing at Campbellsville College, said the school was an important part of Stewart's life. She was deeply committed to the school, he said.

Winters and his wife, Whitt said, were like parents to Stewart.

Stewart was known as a methodical secretary with a penchant for perfection.

Dabney said one of the letters she left spelled out in detail the arrangements for her funeral which was yesterday.

Her work so impressed John Frazer, president of the Association of Independent Colleges and Universities, that he set about to hire her. He was able to do that in July.

Frazer accompanied Stewart to Campbellsville College's Heritage Day on Wednesday, Sept. 21 during which she presented Winters a scrapbook with mementos from his first years as president. The back of the book contained empty pages to fill with mementos yet to come.

A native of Campbellsville, Stewart served as Winters' executive secretary since 1988. Prior to Winters' arrival at the college as president, she served as secretary to Dr. W.R. Davenport, president of the college, from 1984-1988.

Stewart graduated from Campbellsville College in 1974 and in 1981 went to work as secretary to former business vice president J. Alvin Hardy.

In a prepared statement delivered to faculty and staff at 9:15 a.m. Thursday by vice president Dr. Ron Ellis, Winters said, "We are deeply saddened and shocked by this horrible incident. Judi was wholly committed to Campbellsville College and its mission to provide students with a Christian education. Her loss is both a personal one for me and this institution, as well as a professional one."

Stewart's parents are deceased. Survivors include two sisters, Sarah Hubbard and Linda Roots, and a brother, W.L. "Sonny" Stewart, who live in Campbellsville. A complete obituary appears on page 13 of today's newspaper.

Whitt said he saw and spoke with Stewart the day before she died. She had held Whitt's baby.

"She was smiling," Whitt said. "She seemed happy."

A look at the basics
Who
Judi Stewart is the subject of the story.

What
The story is about Stewart's suicide. It includes as many details as possible without being sensational.

When
The time is now. The story was published in a twice-weekly newspaper and that resulted in it appearing the day after Stewart's funeral.

Where
The office of the president of Campbellsville College, a private Baptist school, was the location of the suicide. Stewart's death affected the entire community and the entire college family which encompasses a wide geographic region.

Why
The story only hints at why. It perhaps raises more questions about the why than it answers. Sometimes that's the case when suicide is involved.

How
The how of the suicide is not emphasized. How Stewart's death affected others is. That's perhaps the best way to approach such a story.

Who cares
The entire college family and most of the community cared. Many knew Stewart. Suicides often leave an entire community wondering what could have been done to prevent such a tragedy.

Sources
The coroner, police and a spokesperson for the college were obvious sources. It was also important to talk with those who knew and loved Stewart. Most wanted to talk. They wanted people to know that this was a tragedy.

Another newspaper was also used as a source. Avoid using other media as sources when possible. If it is necessary, attribute the information.

Etc.

Writing about a suicide is never easy. It's especially difficult if you know the victim and others close to the situation. I was greatly concerned about public reaction to the story. No one I am aware of questioned the fact a story was written. One person told me that Stewart was portrayed with compassion.

Another expressed the hope that by trying to understand why someone would commit suicide we might help prevent others from taking their own lives.

It wasn't easy for me to include this story in a book on writing. The fact is that such stories do happen and they often need to be told. That doesn't make it any easier for the reporter covering the story.

Act with compassion and sensitivity. I don't think anyone can ask for more than that.

Chapter 9
Opinion writing

A co-worker once told me that she always has difficulty coming up with ideas for columns. That's a problem I've never had.

Give me 15 minutes and I'll write you a column.

Some might say that proves I'm full of "it," whatever "it" is. Some might also say that I keep up with what's going on in my community and take the time to consider the issues.

A column can generally be defined as the opinion of the writer. It may detail something that has happened to the writer or merely offer a personal view on a matter of general interest.

An editorial is the opinion of the newspaper.

I've always had a bit of a problem understanding exactly who the newspaper is. The newspaper is not a person; it takes many people in fact to publish one. Thus, how can a newspaper have an opinion?

Many newspapers solve that problem by appointing an editorial board. That board may consist of representatives from all departments at the newspaper. Meeting on a regular basis, members discuss the issues of the day and how the "newspaper" feels about those.

The board decides what the newspaper's view is regarding a particular issue.

Someone, usually a member of the editorial board, is then appointed to write an opinion piece reflecting that view.

Most editorials are not bylined. Readers, I suppose, should assume the opinions expressed are those of the newspaper board.

I can't imagine a column without the writer's name. Columns are much too personal for them to be anonymous.

Columns generally are written in first person. Editorials are generally written in third person.

Write about things that interest you but for many reasons may not be appropriate for a news story. Talk about your frustrations with technology or complicated billing systems no one can understand. Write about your personal experiences as a reporter. Tell us what it was like to do something many may never have a chance to do themselves.

Tell us where you stand on an issue. That's something you could never do in a news story but certainly can in a column.

Recognize someone through a column who works behind the

scenes, makes others look good but never gets that accolade he or she deserves. Complain if necessary. Point out situations that could be improved.

Just make sure that over time your columns are balanced. Don't be negative all the time.

Tell us a funny story. Make us laugh. Make us cry. Make us realize you're human. Share part of yourself.

I believe that if you do that, readers will come to know you and respect what you do. Assuming of course that you aren't some type of weirdo that no one possibly could relate to, readers will look forward to your column. They may even read more of your news stories.

For more than 20 years, I wrote a column each week. That's more than 1,000 columns that covered a diversity of topics. I also wrote many editorials.

At the time, there was no editorial board. The managing editor and I usually decided what topics needed to be covered in editorials. We then wrote them, with our names attached.

Some of the editorials took strong stands. The following written by me is one such example:

How bad does it have to get before magistrates act?

Does anyone have a solution better than a tax?

For years I have watched as dozens and dozens of people have paraded before Taylor County Fiscal Court and begged for help. I have also watched as magistrates have collectively shrugged their shoulders and done what they have become noted for — nothing.

Jim Richardson, president of Community Trust Bank, delivered a message to the court Tuesday night that should concern all of us.

Magistrates listened. For a moment, just a moment, I actually thought that someone might do something.

I was wrong.

As usual, the few magistrates who did speak pointed out that no one wants a tax.

Been there, heard that.

It would be unfair to put all of the magistrates in the same sinking ship. Magistrate Gary Osborne is trying to bail out some of the water that is threatening to drown us all, but his lone life preserver won't save us.

Richardson's message was a simple one.

The cost of doing nothing, considering the economic problems the county faces, is much greater than a payroll tax. One need look no farther than Adair County, he said, to learn how important economic development is.

Adair County was already suffering from the closing of the Osh Kosh B'Gosh plant when Fruit of the Loom in Campbellsville eliminated 1,482 jobs. Several hundred of those jobs were held by Adair County folks.

Now, Adair officials must do something to attract jobs. The county has no money to hire an economic development director or to provide the services new industries would demand. Without a new sewer system, no new industry is going to locate there.

Richardson said his bank has already estimated that because of the economic downturn in Adair County, the value of the average home there has declined 10 percent.

Think about that. A home that was worth $50,000 is now worth $45,000, provided anyone would buy it at that price.

A $100,000 home is now worth $90,000. Do the math and calculate what would happen to the value of your home.

Unless something is done in Adair County to turn the situation around, people will begin moving to other areas where there are jobs. Those who decide to stay will find that their children and grandchildren most likely will have to move away to find work.

Such a migration will reduce the tax base, lower tax revenue and forever change a community.

Is that what we want to happen in Taylor County?

Richardson said it can and will unless something is done. The only real option, he said, is a payroll tax. The court has known that for years. So has anyone paying attention.

A 1 percent payroll tax would cost the average worker in Taylor County less than $250 a year.

In return, a full-time economic development director could be hired to recruit new industries, a jail which would employ many and save the county untold thousands of dollars each month could be built, other services could be adequately funded.

This community could become successful again instead of watching silently as night falls.

The average wage would more than likely increase more than $250 a year. The tax would pay for itself and more.

Osborne pointed out during Tuesday's meeting that many of those laid off from Fruit of the Loom have found jobs in the Danville and Glasgow areas. Each of those communities has a payroll tax.

No one there seems to mind paying the tax, Osborne said, and it helps to recruit the jobs that are luring workers there.

He's right, of course.

Taylor County is getting farther and farther behind because county government isn't willing to do what others did long ago.

A tax of $250 per year, less than a buck a day, is little to pay compared to what we stand to lose.

All of us surely don't want to watch our property values decline or our children and grandchildren leave the community to find work.

Magistrate Ed Stamp said less than 10 percent of the people in stores he's talked with support a payroll tax. I wonder where he shops. The only people I've heard talk against the tax are our magistrates. Others seem to realize there is no option.

Magistrate Bobby Roots said Richardson must be new to the community because everyone is opposed to the tax. I wonder what kind of scientifically valid survey he did to come to that conclusion.

I don't like taxes. In fact, I hate them. Most of us hate taxes. Ask people if they enjoy paying property taxes and they will probably say no. But do away with those taxes and we'd all be in a heck of a mess.

Those of us who know there's no option other than a payroll tax need to fill the courtroom each and every time fiscal court meets. We also need to make sure that our magistrates' phones ring off the hook.

Let's prove to them that there are many of us who realize there is no other way out of the mess we're in.

Fiscal court meets again on Nov. 11 at 6 p.m. in the Taylor County Courthouse.

Be there.

Our magistrates are Bobby Kirtley, 465-3754; Edwin

Stamp, 465-6046; Bobby Roots, 465-6837; J.W. McFarland, 465-7627; Marshal Caulk, 465-2174; and Gary Osborne, 465-7465. Fred Waddle, 465-8632, is our county judge.

Call them. Be heard.

Unless our magistrates act, this community is doomed to economic failure. The legacy they will leave is one we certainly don't want for our children.

A look at the basics

Who

The editorial is about Taylor Fiscal Court and the community.

What

The what is the necessity for fiscal court to take action to prevent the economic ruin of the entire community.

When

The time for action is now. The time to talk is over. It's also about the future and the fact there won't be one if fiscal court doesn't act and act soon.

Where

The editorial is about the community and to a lesser extent surrounding communities all facing the same economic crisis.

Why

Without action of fiscal court, nothing will get better. In fact, inaction means property values will decline and people will leave the area to find work.

How

The editorial, as most editorials do, offers suggestions. The suggestion in this editorial might not be popular with everyone but really is the only hope. An occupational tax at a time when many are losing their jobs, the editorial argues, is the only way to save the community.

Who cares

If you lived in Taylor County, you cared. If you didn't care, there definitely was something wrong with you. This editorial talks about survival. You can't get much more basic than that.

Sources

This column was based on my personal observations and quotes from those attending the fiscal court meeting. It also relies on the background I had by attending fiscal court meetings for many years.

Etc.

In a small town it's impossible to work for the media and be anonymous. That means you will likely run into the people you write about at Wal-Mart, Dairy Queen or hundreds of other places.

It can take courage to make strong statements about public officials and then face them eye-to-eye.

As long as you are fair and accurate, I believe in the long run an editorial writer won't face that many problems. In this particular instance, the entire community was tired of waiting for action and turned out in large numbers to demand action.

A tax was finally implemented. An industrial recruiter was hired. Industries came to the area and what could have been the death of the community became a rebirth.

Most members of fiscal court were replaced during the next general election.

Let's be a little less serious and look at a column I wrote about my daughter and Christmas.

Christmas is much more than Santa and Rudolph

One morning last week I asked my four-year-old what Christmas is all about.

She replied by singing about Rudolph the Red-nosed Reindeer and Santa Claus coming to town. Her response was cute, but it did somewhat disturb me.

She did start singing *Away in a Manger*, though, after I started talking about what the day is really all about.

Christmas is a special time of year. And I want it to be a happy time of year for my little girl. It should be a time that children love and look forward to. But I want it to be more than a time of Rudolph and Santa Claus.

I always enjoyed the story of the Three Wise Men following the Star of Bethlehem to the birthplace of Christ. It's a great story. One I personally think is more exciting and meaningful than a television special about the Chipmunks or Garfield and Odie.

Don't get me wrong, I like the Chipmunks and I love Garfield and Odie. But they are not what Christmas is all about.

The continued commercialization of Christmas greatly concerns me. I haven't stopped to count, but I haven't seen many religious displays in stores about the holidays. There are plenty of Christmas trees and Santas, but not as many nativity scenes or Wise Men as I would like to see.

It bothers me that people spend money they don't have buying gifts people don't want to tell them they are thinking about them during the holidays.

Most of us at some point in time have purchased a Christmas gift knowing that the person who will receive it will never use it. Many buys are made just because there has to be a gift for that person under the tree.

And how many of us each year spend money we can't afford to spend? A great many of us, I'm sure.

I enjoy receiving a Christmas gift as much as anyone. But in many instances, a Merry Christmas or a "May God bless your family" would be appreciated just as much if not more than material goods.

I'm not arguing that Christmas shopping cease or that Rudolph and Santa be abolished.

I simply believe that Christ should be put back into Christmas and that some good feelings among men can mean a great deal more than a brightly wrapped present under the tree.

Rudolph and Santa have their good points. They can teach good values to our children as well as love. But they should not replace the love God showed for all of us almost 2,000 years ago on Dec. 25 when he sent a small baby to us who was named Jesus.

That's what Christmas is all about. Rudolph and Santa have their place, but they are secondary to the love that I hope all of us share for each other not only at Christmas but all year.

A look at the basics

Who

Obviously, the column is about my daughter and me. In a much larger sense, though, it is about any parent and child.

What

It's about Christmas and a father's wishes for his daughter. It's about any parent and the hopes and dreams they have for their own children. It's about my belief, and hopefully one others can identify with, that all of us remember what Christmas truly is all about.

When

The column was published just before Christmas. But it also has a message that really is timeless.

Where

The column is about an issue that should concern all of us regardless of where we live.

Why

Details about the Christmas message becoming more commercialized and the fact that bothers this father explain the why. The why in this instance is personal. That reflects the fact it is a column and includes personal views.

How

Again, the how is personal. How the father and daughter react to the seasonal messages and the desire something change make up the how.

Who cares

I'd like to say that anyone with a heart should care about this column. Certainly those who realize the true meaning of Christmas should care. Parents especially should be able to relate to this column.

Etc.

Columns are all about sharing a part of yourself. Some writers don't like to do that. However, revealing some of your inner self in columns and editorials can endear readers and win them over. That can affect the credibility they attach to other stories you write.

Sources

My personal observations and conclusions are at the heart of this column. My daughter also was a source.

The first column I ever wrote was about a Ku Klux Klan rally in Shelbyville. It provides details that are not in the story about the rally and an observation or two. However, it does not offer any *real* opinions.

Perhaps that was the best way to go, though it could be viewed as the coward's way out.

Opinion writing sometimes requires courage. A writer may take stands that may offend or anger others. Though I can truthfully say that no one was ever violent with me because of a column, that possibility certainly exists.

The Klan, just like many others, probably would not have been happy had someone condemned their actions in print. Would there have been any repercussions? There's always that possibility.

You'll have to decide exactly how far out on a limb you want to crawl when writing opinions.

You'll have to also consider whether or not someone might have a saw and cut off that limb on which you have placed yourself.

Here's the column about the Klan rally:

Klan rally was a unique experience

I really didn't know what to expect Saturday evening as I prepared to attend the local rally of the United Klans of America. Night was falling as I arrived at the farm on KY 55, between U.S. 60 and I-64, where the rally was to take place. Several hooded figures greeted me as I approached the gate.

A pickup in front of me contained two young men, both of whom were drinking. Klansmen made the men pour out their liquor and remove their cooler before letting them proceed inside.

My camera was a giveaway which instantly (almost) identified me as a member of the press. I also have a press sticker on my car but the Klansmen asked to see my press pass.

After searching through my wallet I finally found it. I have to admit I was nervous; I had never seen a robed Klansman before.

The men were satisfied I was a member of the press and gave me instructions as to what I could and could not take photos of. In essence, anyone not covering his face had to give permission before I could photograph them.

The Klansmen also asked me if I had any alcoholic beverages or firearms. I replied "no," and was allowed to proceed inside. I parked my car, picked up my camera and began walking in the crowd.

One young man, whose jacket proclaimed him to be a member of the Klan, walked with me toward the speaker stand. He asked me if I had been told about what kind of photos I could take.

I said I had and he disappeared.

In a few moments a gentleman appeared with two robed Klansmen and said they would stay with me all night "for my protection."

I swallowed hard and replied, "OK."

The man whispered to the two and told them to follow me everywhere I went. He also told them about the types of photos I would be allowed to take.

By now it was almost dark and the speakers had begun their appeal for members. I watched as two robed youngsters ran and played in the crowd.

One of my "guards" asked me if I would like a Coke from the nearby refreshment stand.

Eventually the rally was almost over and one of the Klansmen asked me if I would like a membership application. "It's easily done," he said.

"I don't think so," I said.

The finale of the meet was the burning of the cross. I moved closer to get in camera range and my "guards" accompanied me.

One of my hooded accomplices told me the purpose of the cross was "to light up the world for Christ."

The oil soaked rags were wet due to rain that afternoon and the cross would not burn as it should have.

"It usually just goes right up," a woman carrying a small baby said.

The crowd eventually began to break up and the Klan

abandoned its cross which was burning, though not completely.

I told my escorts I was ready to leave and they walked me to my car.

"If you want some more news," one of them said, "some niggers came by waving guns a few minutes ago."

By this time I was at my car. The Klansmen thanked me and one held traffic as I backed out of my parking space. Soon I was on the highway and the rally was over.

A look at the basics
Who
The subject of the column is the KKK.

What
The column focuses on my observations during the rally. It is a descriptive column and does not support nor condemn what I witnessed. Many columns take sides.

When
The rally was a recent event and was in response to other events. Thus, it is a timely column.

Where
Since the rally happened in Shelbyville and focused on nearby events, it is local. The Klan, however, is present in all states.

Thus, the column does have relevance for those who do not call Shelby County home.

Why
The purpose of the rally is explained. The column attempts to offer an objective view of what happened.

How
In a sense, the column depicts a slice of life, though it's a life many might prefer to ignore.

Who cares

Those who live in the area cared. Many seemed unaware that the Klan was active in their home community. Members of the Klan also cared.

The fact they cared, they said, is why they had the rally.

Sources

The column is based on my observations.

Etc.

The column paints members of the Klan as "ordinary people" who enjoy Coca-Cola, are concerned about family values and believe there is a need to be organized. It also points out that they didn't tolerate drinking or guns at their rally.

One might even say the column portrays members of the Klan as polite, concerned people.

After all, they did arrange for me to have an escort. And when I left, they helped me get my vehicle out into traffic.

There were children playing. Speakers talked of a need to return to basic values.

The fact the column made Klan members seem so ordinary, so much like the rest of us, could be what concerned so many people. How can we tell if there is a Klan member in our midst?

Our friends and neighbors could be Klan members. We might never know unless we begin talking about racial issues or witness them burning a cross.

I saw people I knew at the rally. One was a fellow member of the Campbellsville Jaycees.

Another was a police officer in plain clothes. To this day I do not know if he was on assignment or there because he supported the Klan.

Perhaps this column gets its strength from the fact it does not offer strong opinions. Rather, it describes the situation and lets the readers make their own judgments.

Do we really know who our neighbors are?

Columns can go places stories cannot. They can provide additional insight, raise questions, offer solutions and lavish both praise and criticism.

They can permit you to get something off your chest.

Don't focus too much on the negative.

Write something positive once in awhile. That makes the bad easier to swallow. You also won't become known as "that person at the newspaper who can never say anything nice about anyone."

My mother used to always say, "You catch more flies with honey than vinegar."

Personal issues may reflect universal truths

The last column I will share was difficult to write for it reflects a time in my life when a very personal loss was at hand. It is about the last few months of my maternal grandfather's life.

Francis Sisk was known to the entire family as "Granddaddy." He died on May 10, 1992 at the age of 93.

The following column about him was published on April 20, 1992, only a few weeks before his death.

As night approaches, memories fill a void

Frost covers the window through which the honey-gold rays of the sun once smiled.

Delicate swirls of ice obscure the vision of children laughing and playing in the distance.

In a dark corner of the room, he sits all alone and stares into the future. The easy chair he loved is empty. The remote control and color television that kept him busy for the last several months are silent.

The pipe that was his constant companion most of his life lies untouched.

His overalls and flannel shirt that he loved so dearly are neatly folded and put away in a drawer. A hospital gown is now his leisurewear, a wheelchair is his throne and the four walls are his world.

He can no longer talk about yesterday or savor the taste of cornbread and beans. His meals are measured in cubic centimeters and delivered by a vinyl tube.

Sometimes when his daughter visits or his wife speaks of the past, his eyes twinkle ever so slightly before he slips back into the night.

Somewhere in his memories, a light spring rain is falling. He's 10 years old and running through a freshly

I took this photo of my granddaddy, Francis Delery Sisk, on his birthday, May 2, 1981. He was born in 1899 and died on May 10, 1992 at age 93.

mowed lawn. He picks his mother's favorite daffodils. She pretends to be angry before hugging him.

Somewhere in his memories, he's still a young boy running through a field of clover. Close behind him is Old Sam, the hunting dog he raised from a pup.

Somewhere in his memories, he's holding hands with the young girl who lives down the road. He's embracing her and they share their first kiss.

Somewhere in his memories, he's dressed in his best suit. That young girl is now the most beautiful woman he has ever seen. They vow to love one another forever.

Somewhere in his memories, he's pacing nervously in a waiting room, chewing on his pipe. A nurse summons him to his wife's side. She smiles and introduces him to their newborn daughter.

Somewhere in his memories, he's a proud new papa smiling brightly as his daughter takes her first steps.

Somewhere in his memories, he's holding his wife's hand, sharing a kiss, while they watch their daughter dancing with her husband.

Somewhere in his memories, he's standing in front of a glass window looking into the hospital nursery at his newborn granddaughter.

Somewhere in his memories, he's dressed once again in his best suit. Beside him is his still beautiful wife. They are celebrating their 75th anniversary.

Somewhere in his memories, there is no pain. The sun is smiling and he can hear the sound of children laughing and playing.

The frost grows thicker on the window as night begins to fall.

A look at the basics
Who

Though he is never identified, the column is about my grandfather. It, however, most likely reflects the experiences of many. In a real sense, I believe, it shares universal truths many can relate to in regards to their own loved ones.

What

The story is the last few weeks of my grandfather's life. It's about memories, memories we should all cherish. It's about time and the experiences that make life worthwhile.

When

The column was written about a month before my grandfather's death. It details the past and hints at what's to come, something all of us must face eventually.

Where

It's a local column because it's about my grandfather. But it's also one of those universal columns that can be applicable to many people regardless of where they call home.

Why

Writing the column helped ease the pain I faced watching my grandfather's death approaching. It detailed why people mean so much to us.

How

Through descriptions of ordinary, yet powerful, events in a person's life the column speaks about what's most important in life.

Who cares

I did. So did my family. Many readers also did. Several called to tell me how much the column reminded them of a departed loved one. If your readers have any human feelings, they will care about columns such as this.

Sources

This column is deeply personal and is based largely on my observations and memories. My mother also provided a few details.

Etc.

Some may not be comfortable sharing such personal experiences. Most readers react positively to such columns. They can relate to similar experiences.

"Somewhere in his memories" is used to introduce several sentences. That's done for effect. The conclusion also relates back to the lead. That's also done for effect.

The lead describes the rest home where granddaddy spent the last few weeks of his life. There was indeed frost on the window and children were laughing and playing in the distance.

He could not hear them.

This column is not written in the inverted pyramid style. While there are hints throughout the column that death is approaching, that fact is not apparent until the last sentence. That sentence talks about the frost growing thick on the window and night beginning to fall – all references to death.

There's also an earlier reference to no pain, a smiling sun and children laughing and playing. Those references are intended to reflect what awaits us in heaven. Some might not associate those references to the afterlife. Many I know would and did.

My family asked that I read this column at my granddaddy's funeral. I couldn't. The minister who officiated read it. Many family members asked for copies to keep in scrapbooks.

The column reflects my view of my granddaddy. It may not be 100 percent correct for that reason. It reflects the memories I have of him and those that I will forever cherish.

What would you rather be remembered for – columns like this or hard news stories about crime and violence?

Don't be afraid to show that you are human. The best writers and reporters, in my opinion, are human and focus on subjects that reflect that caring. Just remember that personal opinions should only appear in columns or editorials.

You can care about the folks featured in other types of stories. That's OK, I believe, and even desirable. Just include only the facts.

If you can't resist offering your opinion, write an editorial or column. Columns and editorials provide an outlet for many writers that other types of writing simply can't.

A fellow Landmark employee, who works at a newspaper in Tennessee, once told me that he read my column on a regular basis. He said he enjoyed my writing and quite often wanted to reprint some of my columns in his paper.

The only problem, he said, was that my columns almost always focused on Taylor County. Thus, they were not suitable for a newspaper in Tennessee.

The comment was intended as praise. And I took it that way. A writer should write about his own community. People want to read about what's happening to them.

The best advice I can give is to keep your writing local.

Writing editorials and columns sometimes requires courage. People often don't want to read about bad things happening in their community. There are those who prefer not to face reality.

How can we eliminate something that is bad if we don't first recognize that it exists? Newspapers have a responsibility to tell it like it is.

Be courageous.

Chapter 10
Investigative stories

It was a busy afternoon at the Central Kentucky News-Journal, one of the busiest I had experienced in quite sometime.

I had two stories to write, four to edit, several people to telephone and numerous pages to lay out before my day would be over. The last thing I needed was a visit from a distraught reader who wanted me to investigate what she considered to be a travesty of justice.

The only thing going for me was that the woman wasn't upset or angry with me. That would change several days later.

The woman was Linda Colvin and she was understandably upset. She deserved my attention and she got it. In fact, I spent much of my spare time over the next couple of weeks investigating what she shared that busy afternoon.

Colvin's son, James Orberson, had been killed four months earlier. Denise Orberson, his wife and Colvin's daughter-in-law, had been charged by police with murder, but the Taylor County Grand Jury had refused to indict.

Colvin wanted to know how a woman could admit to killing her son and not face murder charges.

I gathered all of the information possible from Colvin and promised I would find out what I could. As it turns out, the story that I was able to assemble was far from what she wanted.

The truth about what had happened between her son and daughter-in-law was not pretty.

It's difficult for reporters at a small paper to do investigative stories. Many smaller newspapers have only one reporter and producing enough copy to fill each issue usually requires all available time.

Large newspapers, logically, have more reporters and can usually find the time to do some investigative stories.

I made phone calls to various sources whenever a spare moment presented itself.

One of the first calls was to the police. I wanted a copy of the police report that was filed when James Orberson was killed. A police officer told me to check the circuit clerk's office for the report and some related paperwork.

That seemed a bit curious since police reports are usually on file at the police station.

The police report was indeed on file in the circuit clerk's office as was a transcript of the interrogation of Denise Orberson. In that transcript, she acknowledges stabbing her husband. She also claims that he came home drunk, began cursing her and hit her in the head with a coffee cup.

The report and the copy of the interrogation were all public record. Any and all parts of either could legally be incorporated into a story. In fact, any member of the public who wanted to see the records could.

A check of other records in the Taylor County Courthouse revealed that James Orberson had been charged several times prior to his death with assaulting his wife. A protective order had been issued against him but was amended shortly before his death.

A conversation with the coroner confirmed the manner in which Orberson died. It also confirmed that he was legally intoxicated at the time of his death.

Who are your other sources?

Both the prosecuting and defense lawyers for the case were contacted. Neither said much, since the matter was technically still pending. They, however, did add to the story as you will discover when you read it.

The defense attorney suggested consulting public records in Marion County. That took a little additional time, and I actually relied on someone at the newspaper there to do the search.

(The Lebanon Enterprise, the newspaper in Marion County, is owned by the same company that owns the Central Kentucky News-Journal. We quite often assisted each other on stories when possible.)

I didn't get the information until after the initial story was published July 9, 1998. Court documents there, as it turns out, were even more revealing.

James Orberson had been charged with assaulting Denise Orberson there, the place they called home before moving to Campbellsville. He also had been charged with assaulting his mother, Linda Colvin.

Denise Orberson could not be reached. Her attorney refused to provide a telephone number or any other method of contacting her.

While it would have been great to have talked with members of the grand jury, such deliberations are, by law, secret. Only indictments – legal accusations – that the grand jury might return are public documents.

Only members of the grand jury would ever know why they decided to not return an indictment.

Read the story and consider the interviews that were necessary to put it together and also decide for yourself if an indictment was warranted:

Mother: Why no indictment?

Grand jury so far hasn't acted in son's stabbing death

Four months after her son was stabbed to death, Linda Colvin doesn't understand why a Taylor County Grand Jury won't indict her former daughter-in-law.

On March 8, Colvin's son, James Orberson, who would have been 24 on July 23, died at his home on Wickliffe Avenue after being stabbed in the heart once with a steak knife. His wife, Denise Orberson, 29, was charged with murder.

The arrest report, on file in the Taylor Circuit Clerk's office, states "Orberson admitted to stabbing her husband with a kitchen knife—causing his death."

Also on file is an interview Campbellsville Police Detective Ron Mann and Patrolman H.W. Nunn conducted with Denise Orberson shortly after James Orberson's death. In that interview, Denise Orberson describes a fight that she said led to the death of her husband.

Denise Orberson, in that interview, says James Orberson came home drunk on March 8, began cursing her and hit her in the head with a coffee cup. She says she threatened to call police and leave the home.

James Orberson blocked her way, Denise Orberson says in the interview. She admits picking up a knife and stabbing him.

(Excerpts from that interview follow this story.)

Taylor County Coroner Terry Dabney said the autopsy report concluded that James Orberson died of a single knife wound to the chest that tore the heart and left lung.

Dabney said James Orberson's blood alcohol level, according to the autopsy report, was 0.15.

"He was legally drunk," Dabney said.

Court records show that James Orberson, during the months preceding his death, had been charged numerous times with assaulting Denise Orberson.

No charges have ever been filed against her.

In April, the grand jury heard evidence in the case but didn't return an indictment or dismiss the charges.

"It takes nine votes to indict or dismiss," Commonwealth's Attorney Barry Bertram said last week. "The case remains in limbo."

That doesn't sit well with Colvin.

"I'm upset about it," Colvin said. "If she doesn't get something for this, what is there to stop other women from killing their husbands and claiming they were abused?"

Colvin said she wants a trial so the complete story of what happened can be told.

Should new evidence become available, it could be presented to the grand jury, Bertram said. He said it would also be possible to submit the case again when another grand jury is seated in January.

Anyone can present evidence to a grand jury, Bertram said, adding that Colvin could appear if she desires.

Though the charges against Denise Orberson are technically still pending, she is free and under no bond. State law requires that the bond for anyone not indicted within 60 days after an arrest be returned.

"The case was fully presented to the grand jury and the grand jury did not indict," said Steve Mirkin, an Elizabethtown public defender who is representing Denise Orberson.

The grand jury, Mirkin said, apparently did not believe that a crime had been committed.

Mirkin was hesitant to comment on the case or Colvin's contentions.

All one has to do, Mirkin said, is look at the court records in Marion County and the assault charges that had been filed against James Orberson.

The fact the charges have not been dismissed doesn't limit Denise Orberson's rights or affect her in any way, Bertram said.

Mirkin agreed.

"It is not an issue," Mirkin said.

Campbellsville Police Chief Terry Gray said the investigation into James Orberson's death remains open.

"It will be an open case until it is solved," Gray said. "The grand jury did not resolve it."

The case likely won't go before the grand jury again, Gray said, unless there's new evidence to present. Leads are being pursued, he said, but there's nothing new at this point.

Gray said he's not certain what happened and many members of the grand jury apparently weren't either.

Denise Orberson could not be reached for comment.

Colvin said her son had been ordered to go to counseling but was killed before the couple's appointment.

"She didn't give him a chance," Colvin said. "I just want some justice."

Police interview provides some details about stabbing

The following is part of an interview with Denise Orberson conducted by Campbellsville Police Detective Ron Mann and Patrolman H.W. Nunn shortly after James Orberson's death and is part of the public record on file pertaining to the case at the Taylor County Courthouse:

"He come in drunk and started hitting on me," Denise Orberson says.

"Started hitting on you?" Mann says. "What happened with the green coffee cup?"

"He was just…he hit me once with it and then he threw it at the stove," Denise Orberson says.

"He hit you in the face with it?" Mann asks.

"He hit me in my head with it," Denise Orberson replies.

"Where was he at when you cut him?" Nunn asks.

"In the downstairs living room," Denise Orberson says.

"…kitchen. In the kitchen?" Nunn asks.

"That's right," Denise Orberson says.

"What did you stab him with?" Mann asks.

"A knife," Denise Orberson says.

"What kind of knife?" Mann asks.

Denise Orberson's reply is unintelligible.

"Where did you get it at?" Mann asks.

"Out of the sink," Denise Orberson replies.

"What happened after you stabbed him?" Nunn asks.

Denise Orberson's reply is unintelligible.

"So after you stabbed him, then what happened?" Mann asks.

"I grabbed my little girl off the couch and..." Denise Orberson says.

"Ran out the back door?" Mann asks.

"Yeah," Denise Orberson replies.

"So you don't know where he went after you stabbed him there in the kitchen? What did he say?" Mann asks.

"He just said ouch," Denise Orberson replies.

Denise Orberson in the interview says she and her husband had amended their "domestic violence papers" a few days earlier and were getting back together.

Then, she says in the interview, James Orberson came home drunk.

"He started cussing and calling me names and saying that I hadn't been home all day and I had been sitting there all day waiting for him to come home," Denise Orberson says.

"He said he ought to knock my brains out and...kill me. I said Jamie I don't want to fight and fuss and he kept on saying come on and hit me. I said I don't want to fight you. And he just kept on and on and then he started ... grabbed the coffee cup and hit me on the side of my head."

A look at the basics
Who

The story is about a mother's grief and her quest for what she calls justice. It also focuses on an abused woman and the husband she eventually killed. In many respects it is not an unusual or uncommon story at all.

What

It's about violence, death and justice.

When

This is a contemporary story, written four months after a young man's death. It could have been written at almost any time, though, about many similar situations.

Where

The story is set in Campbellsville. Again, though, it's one of those kinds of stories that could have happened almost anywhere.

Why

A history of violence, drinking and many other factors all contributed to the death of the young man. The story details that, and one might infer that the grand jury must have considered the death to be justifiable.

How

A major part of the how is told in the daughter-in-law's own words through a police interview. The story also describes how an arrest failed to lead into an indictment and how the grand jury may have viewed the issue. It also describes how the mother feels and her belief that justice was not served.

Who cares

The story was of concern, obviously, to those directly involved. The stabbing of a man by his wife surely is of concern to all of us. Spousal abuse and its tragic results should be also.

Sources

Information for the story came from Linda Colvin, police officers, police reports, numerous other public documents, the coroner and the prosecuting and defense lawyers.

Etc.

Linda Colvin was not pleased with the story. She didn't understand why it was necessary to report her son's past behavior or the fact he was intoxicated. After all, she said, her son was dead. Why was it necessary to smear his name?

A story has to be fair and balanced.

While Denise Orberson admitted stabbing her husband, James, to death, the evidence supported claims of spousal abuse. The coroner also acknowledged that James Orberson was legally intoxicated at the time of his death.

The facts also indicated that James Orberson had a violent temper. Are all of those facts important to present an accurate picture of what happened the day James Orberson was killed?

Yes.

Do those facts at least partially explain why a grand jury refused to indict?

Probably.

Must all of those facts be in the story?

Absolutely.

While the story may have originated because of Linda Colvin, it was not her story. As a reporter, you must seek the truth. The truth sometimes isn't pleasant and may be far from pretty.

I normally put the word truth in quote marks when I discuss what it is. That's because one person's "truth" may be vastly different than someone else's "truth."

Linda Colvin believes her son was murdered and her daughter-in-law got away with it. That's her "truth."

Denise Orberson believes she had no choice other than to kill her husband. That's her "truth."

The police sent me to public records that revealed more than public records usually reveal. Was there a "truth" police believed and wanted to convey?

Of course, the prosecutor and defense lawyers for the case each had their own version of the "truth." What ultimately mattered, though, was the "truth" as perceived by the grand jury.

Everyone has car insurance, right?

Kentucky State Law requires that every registered vehicle carry minimum insurance coverage. In fact, it is impossible to license a car without proof of insurance.

The idea is to assure citizens that if they are injured or their property is damaged, the person responsible will bear the cost.

County clerks who license vehicles, insurance agents, police and county attorneys take the requirement seriously.

Why then are there so many drivers on the road without insurance?

How ironic is it that an insurance agent's vehicle was struck by a car driven by an uninsured motorist?

I don't remember what led me to do a story about uninsured motorists. Perhaps it was because I know the insurance agent who became a victim of an uninsured motorist. It is certain that uninsured motorists cost law-abiding citizens millions of dollars each year.

It is a problem that deserves the public's attention. Let's look at that story:

Uninsured Motorists

Though law requires auto insurance, many don't have it

When Ken Keltner turned his car into the parking lot at his insurance office on Broadway a little over a year ago, he became a statistic.

Keltner's vehicle on that day was "rammed" in the side by a motorist who at first appeared to have auto insurance.

Police responded to the accident, Keltner said, and took all of the necessary information from both drivers. The driver who struck Keltner's vehicle presented a proof of insurance card issued by another local agency.

Keltner later learned that the man's policy had been cancelled three days earlier, and the man had no other auto insurance. After learning the man had no job, lived in public housing and had three children to support, Keltner decided not to pursue the matter and absorbed the cost of repairs to his vehicle.

"I decided not to report him because that would have created a hardship on his family," Keltner said.

Despite the fact that state law requires all motorists to have minimum insurance, many still do not, according to Keltner.

Ray Altman with Smith-Altman Insurance estimates that as many as 20 percent of all drivers do not have required insurance. Altman, who is also a state representative, said the system has been abused for so long that getting a handle on it could be difficult.

Doug Caulk with Caulk and Eastridge Insurance Center said he's had many clients who have been involved in accidents with uninsured motorists. Those who do have insurance, he said, in one way or another end up paying for those who don't.

"There is no free lunch," Altman said.

Altman said insurance companies work on a "pool" system and if someone doesn't put a dollar in, someone else has to put in more.

A vehicle can't be licensed unless proof of insurance is

shown at the county clerk's office.

Obtaining a proof of insurance card, however, sometimes isn't that difficult. Attempts are being made to make it more difficult to obtain a card solely for the purpose of licensing a vehicle.

"I've had people come in and buy insurance, go get their license plate and come back and cancel," Keltner said.

Caulk said he's also had people come in during their birth month- the month a license plate must be renewed- to buy insurance. He said in many instances the insurance is wanted only long enough to show the card to the clerk's office and get a new license plate.

Many insurance agents are now asking potential customers before they will issue a policy where they last had their business. If they haven't had insurance before, Keltner said, a policy either won't be written or they will be referred to "high risk" insurance offered throughout the state.

Such insurance carries a substantially higher premium than regular insurance, Caulk and Keltner said.

Altman said insurance companies are required to send a notice when a policy is cancelled to the Kentucky Department of Motor Vehicle Licensing.

At one time, Taylor County Clerk Randall Phillips said, a list of those who had cancelled was sent to his office as well as the county attorney's office. He said that's no longer true.

Taylor County Attorney Larry Noe said the lists proved to be a paperwork nightmare because notices were sent if a policy was cancelled because someone switched insurance companies.

Phillips said the list still goes to the state and it's up to the Department of Motor Vehicle Licensing to enforce mandatory insurance on vehicles.

The system hasn't worked as well as many had hoped, Phillips said. He said his office can only ask for proof of insurance at the time the vehicle is licensed. And he said he has no way to check to determine if the policy remains in force after the license plates are issued.

It would be possible to require that the annual insurance premium be paid at the time a vehicle is licensed, Keltner said. He said there would be problems in collecting premiums and administering such a requirement.

Noe said some people may continue to drive without insurance or even a driver's license no matter what is done.

He said police do check proof of insurance at roadblocks and traffic stops, but the odds are someone will get away without having insurance.

Keltner pointed out that even those who have the minimum insurance required by the state may not have all they need.

The state, Keltner said, requires limits of only $25,000 per person for bodily injury and $10,000 for property damage. A maximum of $25,000 for medical bills isn't much today, he said, and $10,000 for property damage wouldn't come close to paying for many cars.

A look at the basics

Who

The story is about the people harmed by uninsured motorists. The story is personalized by telling it partially through Ken Keltner, an insurance agent who had to pay for the damage to his own car because the person responsible was not insured. The who could be any of us.

What

The story is about the consequences of driving without insurance and the cost to responsible drivers and society.

When

The story is timely because it is about a problem that exists and has for some time.

Where

It is a local story, though it could have been written anywhere in the state.

Why

Uninsured motorists can destroy their victims physically and financially. That's why we should be concerned.

How

The story describes how motorists can get around the law. It also suggests how the problem might be eliminated.

Who cares

If you drive in Kentucky, you should care. It could be you facing thousands in vehicle repairs or medical bills; and the person who is responsible could very well have no insurance and not a cent to his or her name.

One insurance agent estimated that 20 percent of all drivers are not insured. That's a scary thought.

Sources

Insurance agents, one of whom had been a victim of an uninsured motorist, were sources. So were the county clerk and county attorney. It would have been great to have talked with an uninsured motorist. As you can imagine, finding someone who would admit to driving without insurance wasn't possible.

Etc.

This wasn't an "exciting" or "glamorous" story, but I think it was an important one. In fact the story won an award from the Kentucky Press Association for Investigative Reporting.

There are many problems all of our communities face. Taking the time to look at them is a service newspapers can provide.

This story took a bit longer to do than average. It did not require an excessive amount of time, though, and was mostly done by telephone. It would have been great to have searched public records and determined exactly how many accidents occur each year involving uninsured motorists.

It was written before most records were computerized. Those statistics would likely be easier to obtain today.

The lead personalizes the story by describing the problem one local person had. There's a touch of irony since he is an insurance agent and his car was struck within sight of his office.

Use real people to tell your stories.

Ken Keltner is fairly well known in Campbellsville. If something like this could happen to him, odds are it could happen to almost anyone.

The price of a miracle

When my wife and I had our first and only child, our world

changed. All parents know what I'm talking about. Having children changes your view of the world in more ways than I could possibly describe.

That changed view led to another investigative story.

Almost every physician at one time delivered babies. That's not so anymore. The cost of insurance and the risk of a lawsuit are far too great. That has resulted in an increased caseload for obstetricians who also face skyrocketing costs for malpractice insurance.

Some small communities consider themselves lucky to even have a physician. Those who do not have obstetricians locally most likely must travel to a larger community, or even a major city, to have a baby.

Campbellsville is fortunate enough to still have obstetricians, but their world has changed greatly because of trends in the medical world. Here's the story:

Caseload for obstetricians increases as other doctors quit delivering babies

Almost 500 times each year, Dr. Robert Shipp and Dr. Lewis Cornelius share what many consider a miracle.

Shipp and Cornelius are obstetricians. And last year they delivered almost 500 babies born to mothers from a seven-county area.

Largely because of the cost of malpractice insurance, general practitioners in Taylor, Green, Adair, Russell, and Casey counties no longer deliver babies.

A few in Marion County still bring babies into this world. But many expectant mothers from Marion and Washington counties are delivered by Shipp and Cornelius.

The two obstetricians are also getting Medicaid patients from LaRue County.

"It (the cost of malpractice insurance) has scared general practitioners off," Shipp said. "There's the worry about being sued, there's lots of pressure, there's the cost and there's night work.

"A baby can come at anytime. A general practitioner sees almost every kind of ailment there is and is very busy."

A general practitioner can expect to pay between $8,000 and $19,000 per year for malpractice insurance. An obstetrician actually pays more.

"An obstetrician pays higher rates because it's his specialty," Shipp said. "As a specialist, we are supposed to do everything right. We get sued more than a family practitioner does."

Shipp said the fear of being sued may be as much of a factor in general practitioners choosing not to deliver babies as the cost of malpractice insurance. Plus, he said, practitioners generally would deliver only a few babies a year, not enough to justify the expense and worry associated with that part of the practice.

One of the problems, Shipp said, is the fact that doctors must have insurance that will cover them until a baby they deliver becomes of legal age. He said a doctor can be held liable for any problems encountered during delivery for that long.

Shipp opened his office in January of 1978. During that first year, he paid $4,500 for malpractice insurance and delivered about 100 babies.

"That number rapidly shot up from there," Shipp said. He said he was delivering about 300 babies per year by himself until Cornelius joined the practice four years ago.

Last year, Shipp and Cornelius, who have never had an obstetrical court action against them, each paid $30,104 for malpractice insurance. Together they delivered about 450 babies.

"Most practices deliver that many babies with four people," Shipp said. "The average practice delivers 10 or 15 babies per month. We've had 40 per month.

"It could reach the point that we couldn't do it," Shipp said. "We've reached a peak now."

Shipp said Karen Wolfe, a certified midwife who worked in Green County for several years, joined the staff in February. It took awhile to obtain hospital privileges which would allow her to use the delivery room.

"She has taken a lot of the workload off of us," Shipp said. "She assists in the office and is doing normal deliveries. If there are any complications, we take over."

Shipp said either he or Cornelius is always on call and ready to assist when Wolfe is on duty. State law, he said, requires that a midwife have a medical director who can take over in an emergency. He and Cornelius serve in that capacity.

Earlier this year, Shipp and Cornelius opened an office

in Marion County, but it closed after only a couple of months.

Marion County doctors were planning to quit delivering babies, Shipp said. He said another obstetrician had been recruited to help cover the office, but he changed his mind about coming to the area.

That, Shipp said, eventually resulted in the closing of the office because he and Cornelius couldn't handle the additional office and caseload.

Should Marion County doctors decide again that they aren't going to deliver babies, Shipp said the resulting caseload could force him and Cornelius to once again look for another partner.

Finding another obstetrician could take time, Shipp said, noting that a new $8 million hospital in Breathitt County has been trying to recruit an obstetrician with a guaranteed salary of $200,000 per year plus paid malpractice insurance and has no takers.

There are fewer doctors going into obstetrics, Shipp said, and those who do generally are not going to rural areas where there's a "tremendous workload."

Many obstetricians and gynecologists are no longer delivering babies, Shipp said. He said they are choosing to instead concentrate on the gynecology part of their practice.

"The whole practice of obstetrics is nothing but pressure," Shipp said. "The care of the patient is of concern as is a healthy baby. You hold your breath that the baby comes out normal. You have to deal with two lives."

Shipp said the fear of lawsuits has probably resulted in many doctors performing unnecessary cesarean sections. The state average is 24 percent, Shipp said, while some hospitals have a rate as high as 50 percent. He said he and Cornelius deliver about "20 or 21 percent" of their babies by cesarean.

The increased caseload, Shipp said, "to some extent" has limited the time that he and Cornelius can spend with patients. He said Wolfe has been of great benefit in that respect.

Obstetrical patients at some point, Shipp said, should see all of the three. He noted that patients come every four weeks during the first trimester of their pregnancy, every two weeks during the second trimester and once a week during the last month.

With Shipp and Cornelius working on a rotating basis, an expectant mother "could get either of us in labor."

Shipp said a woman who is in labor and goes to a hospital which has no one available who will deliver a baby will be shipped to another hospital. A helicopter would be called in if necessary, he said.

Should the baby be on the way and a physician not available who still delivers, Shipp said he didn't know what would happen. A physician who delivers a baby and isn't insured is putting his entire career on the line, he said. He said the problem is serious enough that if something isn't done, Louisville and Lexington could become the only cities with physicians and hospitals which will still deliver babies.

"I would quit obstetrics if malpractice suits started popping up right and left," Shipp said. "I hope to be able to continue to fulfill the need here."

Despite the fact Shipp has delivered hundreds of babies, he still considers birth to be a miracle.

"I have to see it that way or I probably wouldn't still be in the business," Shipp said. "There's something about the sparkle in people's eyes and the joy of having a baby. It's a miracle. And the thanks you get is worth more than if you were getting paid double."

A look at the basics

Who

Dr. Robert Shipp and Dr. Lewis Cornelius are the primary focus of the story. It's representative, though, of any physician who delivers babies.

What

Many doctors are no longer delivering babies because of the stress, the cost of malpractice insurance and the threat of lawsuits. The result is fewer and fewer doctors are delivering babies.

When

The story looks at the past briefly, focuses primarily on the present and considers the future. It's a future that could greatly affect anyone planning to have a baby.

Where

While this is a local story, it is a national issue.

Why

The high cost of insurance, increasing patient loads for those who deliver babies and the threat of lawsuits all contribute to the problem.

How

The result is fewer and fewer doctors delivering babies. That means increased patient loads which impacts the quality of medical care. It also impacts the cost for patients and the availability of physicians. It's quite possible that those having babies might have to travel a great distance for medical care.

Who cares

Anyone having a baby is affected. That's a great number of people. Future implications are great.

Sources

The primary sources were Dr. Robert Shipp and Dr. Lewis Cornelius. If time had permitted, hospitals in a wide area could have been contacted for pertinent statistical data.

Etc.

This story details a potential health care crisis.

Where would we all be if expectant mothers couldn't find physicians willing to deliver their babies?

Today's babies are the adults of tomorrow. Sounds like a cliché, but it's the truth.

Dr. Robert Shipp and Dr. Lewis Cornelius are the primary caregivers for pregnant women in several counties. They were the obvious sources for the story.

Certainly, additional information could have been obtained from public documents, hospitals and others.

That would have taken much more time. Would the effort have added enough to the story to have made it worthwhile?

A small newspaper with a small staff most likely could never have spent the additional time required. I personally doubt the story would have much more meaningful had Dr. Robert Shipp and Dr. Lewis Cornelius not been the only sources.

The story was written in the 1980s. It's interesting that WHAS

Television in Louisville did an investigative report on the same subject in 2004.

All newspapers can do investigative stories

An investigative story doesn't have to take weeks or months to research. It is possible to write such stories and still complete routine assignments.

Look for issues or problems that affect your community. Think of ways to explain the situation, possible solutions and the root causes. Find sources. Make a phone call today, another next week and maybe even another next month.

Eventually, you should have the information you need for even the most complicated of stories.

These stories may not win a Pulitzer Prize or anything else. They might, however, point out some problems and offer suggestions that could improve life for those who live in your community.

That would make the effort worthwhile.

Chapter 11
Controversial stories

Sooner or later something you write will upset or anger someone. Count on it.

You might offend one person, two or, perhaps, the entire community. Some stories just seem to bring out the worst in people. Telling the "truth" isn't always popular and you may end up being blamed for what's perceived as offensive or otherwise bad news.

In ancient Greece it was common to kill the bearer of bad tidings. Fortunately that tradition isn't practiced anymore or there would be few stories of any kind.

Even if you're not killed for writing things many would rather not read, the controversy can still be difficult to handle.

A story in The Sentinel-News about a planned abortion clinic was probably the most controversial I have ever written. A few readers called in to cancel their subscriptions after reading "that filth."

One reader wanted to know why my story didn't condemn abortion and everyone associated with the planned clinic. A doctor, who had just retired and whose building was to be used for the clinic, told me that I had "ruined his life."

How do you handle that kind of reaction?

It's not easy. The fact of the matter, though, is that a proposed abortion clinic in a small, conservative community is news. It's BIG news.

A police officer I knew well told me the community should have been grateful that the newspaper found out about the clinic before it opened and told the community. He said his mother was preparing to burn her copy of The Sentinel-News until he made her realize that knowledge can be a powerful thing.

His point is well taken.

How can a community take action to prevent something from happening if they don't know what's planned? How can bad things be eliminated if we prefer to ignore their existence?

After you read the story, I'll continue the discussion about public reaction and its ultimate impact on the community.

Cincinnati doctor plans abortion clinic

A Cincinnati based group, Women for Women, plans to open an abortion clinic on Washington Street in Shelbyville before the first of the year.

From 20 to 30 abortions per week will be performed at the clinic "right off the bat," according to Dr. Robert T. Bliss, who directs a similar clinic in Cincinnati. He said the abortions will primarily be second trimester or up to about 20 weeks pregnancy. Second trimester actually includes pregnancies up to six months.

Bliss said first trimester abortions will be discouraged and only women in the Shelbyville area would probably be considered. The majority of abortions, he said, will be performed on patients from out-of-town.

Bliss said the clinic will "not be a local facility." It will serve the Midwest including Kentucky, West Virginia, Tennessee, Indiana, Illinois and Ohio. He said there is a great demand for abortions in those states.

The clinic will be located at 517 Washington. That is now the Klein-McKee Clinic which is moving to the new professional building at King's Daughters Hospital on Oct. 29. Bliss said he hopes to be in Shelbyville by then to personally supervise the necessary renovation.

Women for Women asked the hospital for permission to perform abortion there, according to administrator Walt Queen.

Bliss said his clinic could open much sooner if permission can be obtained to do abortions at the hospital.

But the executive board of the hospital Friday unanimously decided it is "not interested" in Bliss's proposal to lease space for the purpose of pregnancy terminations. Queen said Bliss only requested to lease space and that nothing was mentioned about using hospital facilities for follow-up after an abortion.

Queen is one of six members of the executive board. Others include: County Judge-Executive Sammy Wood, Nancy Baker, Bob Pearce, Dr. Sidney May and Mary Steuart.

Bliss's request was made in the form of a letter dated Oct. 10.

A lot of work has to be done at the clinic, Bliss said, and using the hospital would be a matter of convenience.

Bliss, who is a gynecologist, said the clinic will deal with women's health and family planning as well as abortions.

Women for Women, according to Bliss, searched a wide area looking for a location for its first clinic in Kentucky. Shelbyville is near Lexington and Louisville where doctors for the clinic will come from, he said. Plus, an existing clinic became available.

No local doctors are involved in the clinic, according to Bliss. He said there will be at least two doctors and probably three. Though he will continue as director of the clinic in Cincinnati, he will also be director of the facility here.

Bliss doesn't plan to move to Shelbyville and will divide his time between here and Cincinnati. Other doctors, he said, might move here but that hasn't been decided. He declined at this time to name physicians who will be working at the clinic.

Kentucky law allows abortions until a fetus is old enough to survive outside the womb. Fox Demoisey, attorney for the Kentucky Medical Licensing Board, said any physician can perform abortions in his office provided he meets state regulations.

For abortions past the first trimester, a hospital or approved clinic is necessary. Demoisey said, "A clinic must have a blood bank, facilities for anesthesiology and resuscitation, and pre- and post- operative care."

A look at the basics

Who

Dr. Robert T. Bliss, a gynecologist who performs abortions, is the main subject of the story and the primary source.

What

The story is about an abortion clinic that plans to open in Shelbyville. This story does not include local reaction.

When

The story appeared in October. The abortion clinic was to open before January. That made the story of immediate interest.

Where

The location is Shelbyville. That's what upset readers. If it had been planned for another city quite some distance away, they most likely wouldn't have been nearly as angry.

Why

Shelbyville is close to Louisville. That means it's close to a major airport in a central location. Bliss said the town was perfect for his clinic because of its location, the fact a medical clinic was available and near hospital facilities.

How

As many as three doctors were to perform 20 to 30 abortions per week. Bliss operates a similar clinic in Cincinnati, Ohio and would be the director. The story details the law regarding abortion clinics and what's legally required.

Who cares

Virtually everyone who lived in Shelbyville cared. The overwhelming majority simply did not want an abortion clinic in their community. Only one person I am aware of said anything after the story broke that could be considered in support of the clinic.

She was a liberal among conservatives. He comment was something to the effect that it was "time Shelbyville joined the 20th century." As you can imagine, her comment was not received with open arms.

Sources

Dr. Robert T. Bliss was the primary source. Information was also provided by Walt Queen, hospital administrator, and Fox Demoisey, attorney for the Kentucky Medical Licensing Board. These sources provided the basic information about the plans for the clinic and what legally was required in Kentucky. For this story, that was probably sufficient.

Stories later on included many more sources including ordinary citizens who were incensed by the idea of an abortion clinic.

Etc.

A rumor about a possible abortion clinic had been circulating for several weeks before the story was written. Many, including me, initially rejected the rumors. No one could, or wanted to, believe the rumors were true.

A check with the county clerk's office in Shelby County revealed a land transfer for the clinic had recently taken place. Such transfers are public record. This particular transfer provided me with the name and address of the purchaser. That led me to Dr. Robert T. Bliss.

Bliss could have refused to talk. Instead, he talked openly about his plans. He apparently had no problem with the newspaper and the community knowing about the clinic. I have to give him credit for that. Many are not so forthcoming.

Reaction to the story was strong and swift. People from all walks of life openly objected to the idea of an abortion clinic. Many called me at the newspaper office and my home to tell me exactly how they felt.

Management of The Sentinel-News decided to give residents a chance to speak out. I was sent to several locations at advertised times to hear comments.

The majority of those were printed in the newspaper.

Bliss ultimately decided that he didn't want to locate his clinic in a community where he wasn't welcome. You could easily argue that the clinic would have been in business before most people knew about it had the story not been published.

The Sentinel-News, I believe, had an obligation to tell the public about the planned abortion clinic.

Still, I believe there are those who would have preferred that a story had never been published. Would they have been happier if Bliss had opened his clinic quietly and few knew what was happening at 517 Washington St.?

The controversy over gay marriages

A story written for the Central Kentucky News-Journal also generated more than its share of controversy. It all began with a short telephone call.

The caller had what I believed to be a legitimate point. At least I thought he had the right to share his beliefs with the rest of the world.

Let me explain.

During the course of a few short months, several somewhat sensational trials involving the sexual abuse of young people had taken place in Taylor County. All of the defendants had been found guilty and sentenced to long prison terms.

Several letters to the editor commented on the sad state of affairs that must exist in a community that permits so much sex abuse to occur. One suggested that a permissive society and media could most likely be blamed.

Another suggested that homosexuals and deviants were at fault.

The caller, who initially would not identify himself, acknowledged he was a homosexual. He was greatly upset by the letters to the editor.

"Homosexuals are not deviants," the caller said. "Being a homosexual does not make one a child molester."

I suggested that the caller could write his own letter to the editor.

"I can't do that," he said. "I'm from Campbellsville. Can you imagine the phone calls my family would get?"

The man eventually agreed to be interviewed for a story. His life partner also agreed. Both requested that their names remain anonymous. They were afraid, for themselves and their families.

The use of anonymous sources, for the most part, should be avoided. There are serious credibility issues. Reporters, unfortunately, have made up sources, quotes and entire stories. Sometimes, however, the use of an anonymous source can be justified.

This was one of the few times in 26 years that I didn't identity my sources. I knew who they were and I understood why they wished to remain anonymous.

Many in the community objected to the story and wrote nasty letters to the editor. One actually was grateful. That person, a woman, said the community needs to have understanding and compassion for others.

A newspaper colleague told me that on occasion it is necessary to "push the envelope" and tell readers some of the "truths" about the place they call home. There may be "truths" that some don't want to acknowledge, he said, but nevertheless they are part of our world.

My intention in writing the story was not to be sensational or to create a stir. It was to give two sincere people a chance to offer their opinions on what admittedly is a controversial subject.

Did it contribute in any way to understanding?

I don't know.

It is the story of these two men in their own words.

Here's the story:

Gay couple seeks acceptance

Homosexuals aren't perverts, Campbellsville native says

Editor's Note: The names of the individuals in the following story have been changed to protect their identities.

Sam is in love for the first time in his life and would love nothing more than to get married.

But Sam knows that his family would never accept his marriage. Many of his friends probably wouldn't either.

That's because the love of his life, the person he would like to marry, is David, a man he has lived with for a little more than five years.

"There's a lot of prejudice in Campbellsville, especially towards gays," Sam said.

Sam acknowledged that he is only speaking about his lifestyle because of two recent incidents in Taylor County that have negatively portrayed those who are gay.

A man convicted of abusing his stepdaughters, Sam said, in part blamed his actions on the abuse he allegedly suffered as a child by a homosexual relative. He said there's another case yet to come to trial involving a man who allegedly forced young boys to have sex with him.

"A gay person is no more likely to be a pervert or child molester than anyone else," Sam said.

David agreed.

"There is a gay phobia among some people," David said. "There's no reason for it. The only perverts or child molesters I have ever been aware of have all been heterosexual." Many people fear what they don't understand, Sam said. He said he hopes that by speaking about his lifestyle at least a few people will realize that the words "gay" and "pervert" are not one and the same.

"Being gay doesn't bother me, but I don't flaunt it either," said Sam, who is in his early 30s and moved away from Campbellsville several years ago. Most of his family still lives here.

David is from the Louisville area where the couple lives now.

"We're not openly gay," Sam said. "By that, we don't

hold hands or kiss in public. But we feel more comfortable being together near a larger city than we ever would in Campbellsville."

Sam grew up in a middle class neighborhood. As a youngster, he played baseball, took swimming lessons, and played one year of football. In high school, he dated and took a girl to the prom.

"I tried, but I never fit in," Sam said. "Lots of people don't fit in, so that wasn't that unusual. I always knew I was different. I just really never understood why."

After going away to college and living in an environment where he felt more comfortable to be himself, Sam came to terms with his sexuality.

"I always thought I was gay," Sam said. "But that's not something that a teen-ager growing up in Campbellsville would readily accept or admit. I found more acceptance in college and found others like me."

Sam never frequented gay bars. And though he admitted to himself while in college that he was gay, he never had a relationship with a man until he met David about six years ago.

"I never liked gay bars and you won't ever find me in one," Sam said. "There are many who go there looking for something they never find. I was so lucky. I found David. We're alike in so many ways and get along better than most married heterosexual couples I know."

David, who is also in his early 30s, says little. He generally prefers not to talk about the private aspects of his life.

The two met at a Star Trek convention and discovered that they had much in common. A few casual lunches and conversations turned into dates and eventually romance.

Both have good jobs.

A few close friends know of their relationship. Others believe they are only roommates.

"I wish I had the courage to tell people who I am," Sam said. "I don't. I'm not the only gay person who's from Campbellsville. There are gay people there. No one should fool themselves in believing there aren't.

"Campbellsville just isn't ready to accept gay people. I don't want people laughing and pointing when I visit and I don't want people harassing my family."

David says he's been to Campbellsville a few times and likes the community but doesn't believe he and Sam could ever call the town home.

"The community is nice and people are friendly, but I wonder how much that would change if people knew my relationship with Sam," David said.

Both said they hope that some day gay people will be treated just like everyone else.

The fact that someone is gay, Sam said, doesn't make that person bad. He said because someone is heterosexual also doesn't make that person bad or good.

"People should be judged by their character, not by their sexual orientation," David said.

"No one made me gay," Sam said. "I am gay because that's the way I am. You should never try to convince anyone to be something they aren't. People have to be who they are."

A look at the basics
Who

The story is about two gay men, one of whom is a native of Campbellsville.

What

It is the story about what it's like to be gay and not feel comfortable in your hometown, among friends and relatives.

When

The story was timely because it was in response to comments many had made about perverts and homosexuals in relationship to trials at the time.

Where

It was about a former Campbellsville resident who had to leave town to find acceptance of some sort. It was very much a local story, though it was one many did not want to read.

Why

Sam and David came forward only because of allegations that had been made by others regarding perverts and homosexuals. Many asked why the newspaper published the story. One of the basic tenants of journalism is to give voice to the voiceless or, in other words, to ensure that all members of society have a chance to be heard.

How

In the story, Sam and David attempt to explain how homosexuals are loving and caring individuals. They also attempt to explain that, in their opinion, heterosexuals, actually commit most sex offenses.

Who cares

Many cared enough to comment about the story. The overwhelming majority of those comments were negative. Be prepared when writing about something controversial to hear much criticism.

Sam and David cared. They were actually pleased with the story. They believed that if one person might be a little more tolerant because of it, then it was worth it.

The woman who expressed gratitude for the story also cared.

Sources

The story was based entirely on the interview with Sam and David. I have actually forgotten their real names. That, I suppose, was on purpose.

Etc.

If I had it to do over again, I probably would not write the story. The criticism was intense. It's amazing how intolerant people can be in a country that is supposed to be based at least in part on tolerance.

A few thought I should have condemned Sam and David in the story.

Reporters merely serve as the conduit for messages. They should never become part of the message or story.

Readers are a diverse group. If the media adequately covers the groups that make up its constituent base, does that mean stories such as this one are necessary? Or do stories such as this merely emphasis certain realities many would rather ignore?

Did this story enlighten or provide voice to the voiceless?

Would you have written this story?

Is the KKK part of your community?

A story I wrote about the Ku Klux Klan while a reporter for The Sentinel-News also generated more than its share of comments and criticism.

Let me make it clear that I have not, nor have I ever been, a member of the KKK. I was assigned to attend a KKK rally and write the story for The Sentinel-News. I drew the assignment because the rally happened on Saturday and it was my turn to work weekends.

That's the only reason I was there.

This was a "full-fledged" KKK rally complete with a cross burning.

KKK rallies are not common fare in Shelby County. The rally was largely in response to an incident in nearby Louisville involving a black police officer who was suspended for his political views and filed suit claiming, among other things, racism by his superiors.

Let's look at the story:

Klan rallies for members

"This is America: this is where it's happening," the hooded figure said as Saturday's local rally for the United Klans of America got under way.

The purpose of the meeting was to add members to the ranks of the organization. Each speaker expressed his, and the Klan's, discontent with the federal government and concern with what they termed "the decaying morals of the country."

Political involvement, they insisted, is the only way to stop the advance of communism. Foreign aid, the speaker claimed, goes to support communist armies and other groups dedicated to the destruction of the white middle class.

The Grand Dragon of Kentucky (the head of the Klan in the state) spoke of political corruption in many counties. He also spoke of the horror of drug addiction and the need to elect people who will take action to solve the nation's problems.

"I hear you have elected a pretty good slate up here," he told the crowd. "I'm glad to hear some of you people are waking up."

The Klansmen said they believe busing is a plot instigated by communists. One young hooded man, who said he attends school in Jefferson County, told the crowd the opening of school this year will not be as peaceful as officials have claimed.

Still another told the crowd they should become

involved in the Shelby Lanier case. "Niggers are involved in it," he said. "We should see he stays fired."

Lanier is a black policeman who was suspended from the Louisville force after allegedly making a political speech while on duty and in uniform.

Klansmen claimed 98 percent of the new media is controlled by the federal government which is, itself, a part of the "upper arm of communism." They also referred to The Courier-Journal as the "Red Rag."

"The media will continue to pour out untruths," one female Klansman said, "and the Klan remains unknown for this reason."

Anyone from 8 years old and up can join the Klan, spokesmen said. As proof of that statement, youngsters milled about the rally in their robes which declared them to be members of the Ku Klux Klan.

We are concerned and dedicated to Christianity and this nation, a hooded figure emphasized. Join us, if you care about your children, she added.

The same Klansman noted the group does not "hang blacks." Another, however, indicated the Klan would resort to violence if necessary.

The Klan invited those interested to step up to a blue pickup where membership applications were available. Meanwhile, Klansmen prepared to burn a cross. The burning, they noted, is to "light up the world for Christ."

Rains on Saturday afternoon dampened the oil soaked rags and the cross was reluctant to burn. Eventually it did catch fire and the rally was over.

A look at the basics
Who
The story is about the Ku Klux Klan.

What
Specifically, it is a story about a rally and offers the Klan's views on a variety of subjects.

When
It was a Saturday rally and in response to recent events in Louisville.

Where
The site was a field in Shelby County, just outside Shelbyville. It was very much a local story with many local participants.

Why
The rally, according to the Klan, was partially in response to the Shelby Lanier controversy in Louisville. Shelby County is a "bedroom" community for many who work in the nearby city.

How
The rally, according to the Klan, showed support for the organization's cause. It was complete with hooded figures, speeches and a cross burning.

Etc.
None of the Klan members are identified. That's because none of them identified themselves when speaking. Most, wearing Klan robes, had their faces covered.

A column also addressed some of the issues raised during the rally.

There is one omission in the story and column. The size of the crowd is not listed. It should be.

At events, a reporter should attempt to count the number of participants.

At a small event, that shouldn't be difficult to do. At a large event, a reasonably accurate count is still possible. Divide the gathering place into sections, count one section and do that math. That will result in a reasonable accurate total.

To the best of my recollection, the rally attracted fewer than 100 people.

In the overall scheme of things, that's not that many people. What made the rally news, though, was the fact a gathering of the KKK in Shelby County was unusual. I'd also venture it's something most people would want to know about.

The story details how the rally began, some of the comments made and how it ended. There's language that might offend some. It's accurate, and probably what you would expect to hear at such a rally.

I believe it was a necessary part of the story. Some readers took offense to the language. Some were offended that the newspaper would even "legitimize" the Klan by writing about the rally. Interestingly enough, not a single comment about the story was made by the Klan or at least no one who called said they were a member of the group.

Again, some wanted to know why the newspaper didn't point how horrible the Klan is and condemn Klan members for their racist views.

The purpose of a news story is to report the facts – nothing more, nothing less.

Had there been protesters at the rally, that would have been printed. There were none.

A reporter's job is to report what happened. The readers can then decide for themselves if what happened is a good thing, bad thing or something else.

Some stories will be controversial. That's just the way it is.

Chapter 12
Public meetings, the courts

The majority of the world would probably never attend a public meeting unless door prizes of significant value were given away or something was happening that greatly affected them.
Most reporters probably wouldn't either.
Fact is public agencies tax us, pave our streets, install water lines and sewers, pass laws affecting what we can do with our property, build schools, hire teachers, force us to leash our dogs, tell us how loud we can play stereos at night and a multitude of other things.
Public agencies impact our lives. Sometimes they impact our lives greatly.
Most public agencies meet at least once a month. Even in a small community, there are many public agencies – school boards, city council, fiscal court (county government), zoning board, library board, water board and, perhaps, more.
Some counties have more than one city, thus, multiple city councils. Some have more than one school system. If there's more than one school system, there's more than one board.
Even if there isn't more than one school system, there's more than one board that governs schools. Kentucky several years ago created site-based decision-making councils at each school. Those councils make many decisions that boards used to make.
Regardless of how many school systems there are, there will be several schools.
The point is simple, there may be many public agencies in your community that you must cover on a regular basis.
Become familiar with the public agencies in your community. Know what they do. Know when they meet. Know the applicable laws regarding the public agencies in your communities.
In Kentucky, meetings of public agencies are open to the public with very few exceptions. All public agencies are required to have regular meeting times and places. They are also required to notify the public of those times and places and any changes.
Learn who the members of the agencies are. Most are either elected or appointed. They are public officials and have an obligation to be open about their actions. Ask for copies of agendas. Some agencies will

send you copies in advance. Some may not provide them until the time of the meeting.

Not everything a board or agency does is of interest. Problem is most will never tell you when something "good" is going to happen. You've got to be there and hear for yourself.

Even if something "good" does happen, the details may not be spelled out for you. You've got to listen closely and determine what is of importance. Sometimes it's clear. Sometimes it's not.

For example, here's a summary of an agenda for a city school board meeting I covered several years ago:

—Opening prayer.
—Call to order.
—Approval of minutes.
—Approval of treasurer's report including $100,000 in carryover funds from this budget year to the next.
—Report by a middle school teacher on field trip to Actors' Theater in Louisville.
—Purchase of two school buses at a cost of $60,000 each. The buses replace two that are eight years old and due to be retired.
—Employment of Colin McDaniel as a high school English teacher to replace a teacher who was not rehired for next year.
—Adjournment.

What is the most important part of this story? What is the least important?

Do you include everything?

Do you need additional information?

We'll come back to this agenda in a moment.

Arrive at the meetings early. Listen to any pre-meeting conversations. It's amazing sometimes what you might overhear.

If you don't know members of the agency, introduce yourself. Sit close to the members. Members of most agencies usually sit around a table of some sort. If you're lucky, there will be a nameplate or something in front of each member to tell you who is who.

I've been to meetings where members actually sat with their backs to the audience. That made it difficult to know who was saying what.

If something is said that you don't understand, you've got two choices. You can either ask questions during the meeting or wait until after it's over. Generally, I wouldn't interrupt the meeting unless something really needs clarifying right then and there.

It's not unusual to ask a few questions of some of the agency members or the head after the meeting is over. Some additional details or clarification might be necessary.

By asking afterwards, you can also be certain that any other media doesn't hear the same answers. Remember, you do have competitors. Do you want all the other newspapers, radio stations, TV stations, web sites, etc. to know exactly what you know?

Let's go back to the agenda for the city school board meeting and look at the basics.

A look at the basics

Who

In this category you could easily place the members of the city school board, the superintendent, an unnamed middle school teacher and Colin McDaniel, a new English teacher.

What

The board read the minutes, heard a great treasurer's report, heard a report about an educational trip, purchased two school buses and hired an English teacher. The trick is to decide which of these actions is most important.

When

The board met Monday night. The story will appear in Thursday's newspaper. The school buses to be replaced are eight years old. Is any of that significant? McDaniel will become an English teacher in the fall.

Where

The middle school, the high school and even Actors' Theater in Louisville were all discussed. Is any of that really that important?

Why

No reason was given as to why the school system is so well off financially, assuming $100,000 is that significant for when the total budget is several million dollars. The school buses are old and due to be retired. That's another why. No reason is given for replacing the English teacher.

How

The how for this story is very similar to the why. Neither is of that much consequence.

Who cares

Let's determine what's most important about the story before answering that.

The name Colin McDaniel caused me to pay special attention to what otherwise might have been a routine matter.

I asked no questions during the meeting because I did not want to tip off a reporter from the local radio station who was brand new and most likely had never heard McDaniel's name before.

Colin McDaniel just happened to be the name of the Campbellsville Police Chief. I verified with the superintendent after the meeting that this was the police chief who was becoming an English teacher and not someone who just happened to have the same name.

Now, who cares?

You can't be a police chief and an English teacher. The entire community was impacted because a new chief had to be found.

A police chief can greatly impact a police force. And a police force can greatly impact a community.

I was able to contact McDaniel, who didn't want to comment, the mayor and others who would be involved with hiring a new chief. That provided detail for my story.

The local radio station may have had coverage about the meeting before my story ran, but I had the *real* news.

The radio story talked about the purchase of school buses and never even mentioned McDaniel's hiring.

There's a lesson here. If you don't know who someone is, ask. By the way, my lead didn't just say:

> Campbellsville Police Chief Colin McDaniel has been hired as a high school English teacher.

I think it was a little better than that. Here it is followed by the complete story:

City police chief to resign, become English teacher

Campbellsville Police Chief Colin McDaniel will be putting his badge and gun down in August and picking up a high school English text.

McDaniel was hired by the Campbellsville Board of Education Monday night as a high school English teacher for the 1982-1983 term. He will replace Paul Dawson, a first-year teacher who was not rehired last month.

In a telephone interview yesterday, McDaniel refused to comment until he actually signs a contract with the Campbellsville Board of Education.

A contract was ready for McDaniel's signature yesterday at press time, according to Dave Fryrear, superintendent of Campbellsville schools. Fryrear said yesterday that McDaniel has accepted the job, a contract just hasn't been signed yet.

The city school board, according to Fryrear, would not have voted Monday to give McDaniel a contract as a teacher unless he had indicated he would accept. Fryrear said the position normally would not have been filled this quickly, but the board wanted to give the city time to find a new police chief.

Campbellsville Mayor Robert L. Miller said Tuesday that he wasn't surprised McDaniel has accepted a position as a teacher. He said there have been discussions about the possibility.

A replacement for McDaniel would be left entirely up to the police commissioner, according to Miller. He said he hoped a suitable replacement could be found by the time school starts on Aug. 16.

Police Commissioner Frank Metzmeier said the city regrets losing McDaniel. He said it would be hard to find a replacement of the same caliber.

McDaniel had been looking for a teaching position with the city's knowledge, according to Metzmeier. He said the police chief had prepared himself for such a position by completing his teacher's degree.

Two years ago, McDaniel did his student teaching at Campbellsville High School. Fryrear said he did an excellent job and the school system is excited about having him as a teacher.

"If a contract is offered," Metzmeier said, "Colin will accept. It will be with regret on our part. He feels he can be of service to the community and to the children. It will be a loss to the (police) department and to the city."

Metzmeier said a search for a new police chief would begin as soon as McDaniel signs a contract with the school board. He said it would be difficult to find a suitable replacement by August.

The city will be cautious in its search for another police chief, according to Metzmeier. He said careful attention would be paid to finding someone who exemplifies the ideas of the police department.

If at all possible, Metzmeier said, the position would be given to someone either serving now on the police department or someone who has served in the past. He said it would be good for the chief to personally know the members of the department.

A replacement for McDaniel, according to Metzmeier, must possess the proper training, leadership abilities and administrative abilities.

McDaniel has been police chief since late August of 1980. He replaced James Walters who retired after more than 20 years on the force.

Some information gathered at a public meeting simply is excess and has no place in your stories.

If you believe that additional information does belong in the newspaper, there are a couple of options. First, it could be included at the end.

Write the story about what's most important. Then say something to the effect: In other action, the board did such and such. List each item in a separate paragraph or two with some type of bullet to begin each.

If the other items deserve more than a couple of paragraphs, write another story.

There is no rule that mandates only one story per meeting or interview. By writing more than one story, it is possible to keep each to a manageable size. It is also possible to use the most important story on the front page and the least important elsewhere.

Remember Magistrate Bobby Kirtley referred to earlier? He was once a member of Taylor County Fiscal Court. His comments are central to the following story involving fiscal court's reaction to a proposal to merge city and county governments:

Merger vote may be delayed

Voters most likely will not be asked this November if they are for or against a merger of city and county government.

Instead, the question will likely be on the ballot in November 2002.

Taylor Fiscal Court must create a committee to draft a charter for a combined government after being presented a certified petition asking that the question be on the ballot. The court Tuesday night, however, took no action regarding the committee.

The court has 60 days after the certification of the petition to appoint the committee, according to Taylor County Attorney Craig Cox.

The petition was certified on July 12, Cox said, so the court has until Sept. 12 to create the committee and set its size from 20 to 40 members. The court will appoint 55 percent of those members and the city will appoint the others.

Taylor County Judge/Executive Eddie Rogers by virtue of his office would be a voting member of the committee.

Cox said the charter must be completed and published 90 days before an election to be on that ballot. Calculating backwards from the general election in November, he said, the petition must be published no later than Aug. 9.

The closest newspaper date to that date, Cox said, would be Aug. 7. He said the charter would have to be completed several days before that to allow time for it to be prepared for publication.

As a practical matter, Cox said, the committee must be created, all members appointed and a final charter approved within two weeks if the question is to be on the ballot this November.

"We have 60 days to appoint the committee?" Magistrate Bobby Kirtley asked Cox during Tuesday night's meeting of fiscal court.

Cox said that was correct.

A proposed charter, drafted by a committee that has studied the issue of merger and circulated the petitions asking that the question be on the ballot was presented to magistrates at that meeting.

That charter, Cox said, could be adopted by the committee, amended as desired or ignored completely. He said the only issue before the court was the creation of a committee, its size and appointment of 55 percent of its members.

Kirtley asked who led the group that put together the proposed charter.

Dale Furkin, a member of the group, said Steve Doss was the primary organizer.

Kirtley asked what role David Nunery, a local attorney and member of Campbellsville City Council, played.

Furkin said Nunery also had a leadership role.

"Were they born and raised here?" Kirtley asked.

"People who love this county and put their lifeblood into it don't have to be from here," Furkin said. "That is not an issue."

Kirtley also said that Nunery as a member of city council had approved an inter-local agreement with the county calling for occupation tax funds to be used for a jail.

Before a hearing on the jail, Kirtley said he received a letter from Nunery opposing construction.

If Nunery would lie about the jail, Kirtley asked, how could he be trusted regarding merger?

Magistrate Ed Gorin said presenting a charter before a committee is appointed "sounds like putting the cart before the horse."

There was no reason to proceed with anything, Furkin said, if enough signatures couldn't be obtained on the petitions. She said time was also of the essence if the question was to be on the ballot this year.

All of that, Furkin said, is why a committee was formed and a proposed charter adopted. She said all of the meetings were open to anyone concerned and that included members of fiscal court.

"The ultimate last word will be from the people who vote on it," Furkin said. "If it is not going to go on the ballot, a lot of people are going to be hurt."

Kirtley said he believes the idea of merger is all about control, specifically desires that Nunery has.

"Amen," Magistrate James Cochran said following Kirtley's statement.

"In my opinion, this ain't nothing but garbage," Kirtley said. "You shove this junk in our faces and expect us to do it in two weeks. I wouldn't do it for nothing."

"You would deny everyone else a chance to vote?" Furkin asked. "I feel like I am beating my head against a brick wall."

Gorin said he and the court recognize that they must set up the committee "sooner or later."

"There are 52 weeks in the year," Kirtley said. "Why did you wait until there were two weeks and then throw this in our faces?"

Furkin said the issue was not thrown in magistrates'

faces. There have been meetings all along, she said, that any of them could have attended.

"Who wants to go to meetings when you ain't for something?" Kirtley asked.

Furkin said she often goes to meetings to learn more about issues she either knows little about or disagrees with.

"We are not asking you to vote for it," Furkin said. "We are asking for the opportunity for voters to consider it. What have you got to lose by letting the people speak?"

Kirtley asked how much it will cost to publish the charter and who will pay.

Cox said the court will be responsible for 55 percent of the cost and the city will pay the rest.

The court's share, Furkin said, would probably be around $2,500.

Calling Furkin "honey," Kirtley said $2,500 would put about "50 loads of rock on roads."

"If roads are our only considerations, than we need to rethink our priorities," Furkin said. She also asked if Kirtley had called her "honey."

He said he did.

Cox said if the merger question isn't on the ballot this year, it would be on the ballot in November 2002. There is no general election in 2001.

The fact magistrates were elected in 2002 could be an issue, Cox said. A charter form of government cannot put an end to the terms of either magistrates or members of city council. If a merged government were approved in 2002, he said, it might take four years for it to become effective while magistrates' terms expire.

Rogers asked if there were any motions regarding the issue.

The court responded with silence.

Unless a special meeting is called to discuss the issue, it won't be considered again until August. And that would be too late for the question to be on the ballot this December.

Aug. 8 is the next regular meeting date for fiscal court.

A look at the basics
Who

The story is about a regular fiscal court meeting. The major players are Bobby Kirtley and Dale Furkin. Lesser roles are played by Ed Gorin, Craig Cox and Eddie Rogers.

What
The reaction of the magistrates to the proposal is at the heart of this story.

When
The meeting was in July 2000. Action had to be taken immediately if the matter were to be on the ballot that December.

Where
The question affected Campbellsville and Taylor County.

Why
The story does not tell readers why supporters want to merge city and county governments. Previous stories had already done that. It does point out that a couple of magistrates are very much opposed to the idea. Are their reasons really clear?

How
The process necessary to place the question on the ballot is outlined as is fiscal court's role.

Who cares
Kirtley obviously cared very much. Some of the other magistrates did too. There are six magistrates. Some of them didn't say anything. Merger of city and county government should concern all residents of the city and county. It would change the government process and those in leadership positions.

Magistrates could have lost their positions. Could that be why some of them were so opposed to the idea of merger? As it turns out the majority were not re-elected for another term.

Sources
The story is based solely on what happened and was said during the meeting.

Etc.

The meeting was on Tuesday night. The deadline for the story was Wednesday morning. It had to be written, proofed and on the page by 11 a.m. That left little time for additional research, questioning or writing.

While the lead works, in retrospect I should have worked Kirtley's comments into the first couple of sentences. He vocalized what the majority of the court seemed to think.

Notice that the quotes attributed to Kirtley were not "cleaned up."

He said "ain't," and the quotes reflect that. There were also some other grammatical problems with some of what he said.

Quotes should echo what the reader would have heard had he or she been at the meeting.

Is it being unkind or unfair to Kirtley to use quotes with bad grammar? I don't think so. He was a member of county government and, I believe, people have a right to know all they can about him.

Was it fair to point out that Kirtley had called Furkin "honey?"

Again, he was an elected official and the way he treated people was certainly relevant.

Nunery was not at the meeting. If you remember, Kirtley said Nunery was a liar and could not be trusted. Nunery had a right to respond.

Though time was short, an attempt was made to talk with Nunery about Kirtley's comments. He was out of town and could not be reached until after the story was published.

A story in the next issue of the newspaper included his reaction to Kirtley's statements. He was gracious, more so than most people probably would have been. In fact, he said he respected Kirtley's opinions.

Notice that the lead does not mention Taylor County Fiscal Court. It focuses on the essence of the story.

There's no need to mention the fact the story originated at a meeting in the lead. That bit of information has to be in the story somewhere, but it usually can be much farther down in the story.

Many interesting and provocative stories happen at "routine" meetings. You've got to be there, listen carefully and take notes.

Court is now in session

Let's now turn to the court system for a moment.

Covering a trial or other court action is similar to covering a public meeting. Trials are open to the public. They are conducted by public officials.

Don't interrupt during a trial. Sit quietly, take notes and save any questions for recesses.

Disrupt the proceedings and you'll probably be asked to leave.

Public meetings may last for an hour or two or even four. Trials may last for days. There may also be preliminary hearings. Some trials, from the first hearing to a verdict, could take years.

State courts in Kentucky do permit photographs.

Do not use flash. Do not do anything to distract from the proceedings. If you don't know the judge, it would be a good idea to talk to him or her prior to the trial about photography.

You do not want a judge mad at you.

Since trials can last for days, you most likely won't be present for all of the testimony. If you know someone in the court system well enough, you might be able to skip some of the preliminaries.

Jury selection can take hours. That's not something you would likely need to sit through.

Be there for opening arguments by both the prosecution and defense. Find out when "key" witnesses are going to testify and be present for that. Also find out when closing arguments will be made.

The opening and closing arguments sum up the cases for both the defense and prosecution. If you can attend the entire trial, do so.

A contact in the court system can also alert you as to when a jury has reached a verdict. The alternative is to sit and wait in the courthouse, perhaps for hours.

Some trials can be sensational and generate much controversy. Such was the last one I covered. It attracted media from all over the state. It also raised many questions and several ethical issues.

One radio station identified the man by name but not his daughter. If you identify the man, aren't you essentially also identifying the daughter?

Should you identify a victim of incest?

Consider how you would have handled this story.

Jury finds man guilty of raping his daughter

5,640-year sentence may be longest ever in state of Kentucky

A sentence of 5,640 years has been recommended for a 40-year old Taylor County man found guilty of raping his daughter almost every week for three years beginning when she was 11 years old.

The sentence is believed to be the longest ever recommended by a jury in Kentucky, according to Assistant Commonwealth's Attorney John Bertram.

It took a Taylor County Circuit Court Jury 40 minutes late Thursday afternoon to find the man guilty of 150 counts of first-degree rape, 75 counts of first-degree sodomy and one count of intimidating a witness.

The man is not being identified by the Central Kentucky News-Journal to protect his daughter's identity.

It took the jury another 20 minutes to recommend a sentence of 50 years each for 25 counts of first-degree rape, 20 years each for 125 counts of first-degree rape, 50 years each for 13 counts of first-degree sodomy and 20 years each for 62 counts of first-degree sodomy.

Bertram said the difference in sentences for the counts is due to the age of the victim when the offenses occurred. The rape of a child under age 12, he said, carries a longer prison sentence.

The victim was under age 12 during approximately one-third of the rape and sodomy incidents. Bertram said, thus the difference in sentences.

All sentences are to be served consecutively for a total of 5,640 years.

The man was also sentenced to three years for one count of intimidating a witness. The jury recommends that sentence be served concurrently which would result in no additional prison time.

"I have never in my life seen a recommendation that adds up to this many years," Bertram said.

Circuit Judge Doughlas George will formally sentence the man on Sept. 5. Though Bertram said the judge usually follows the jury's recommendation, he's not obligated to do so.

Even if the man is sentenced to 5,640 years, Bertram said he will be eligible for parole in 12 years. Kentucky law recognizes life in prison as the longest sentence possible, he said, and parole in 12 years is still possible for that offense.

During the sentencing phase of the trial, Bertram said the jury was asked to set a long sentence as a message to the parole board that the man needs to remain in prison for what he did. A sentence of 5,640 years might seem outrageous, he said, but there's a reason for it.

"The more outrageous it is, the more likely the parole board is going to take notice," Bertram said.

The man originally was charged with only one count of rape and one count of sodomy, Bertram said. He said the man entered the plea and a sentence of 10 years was recommended.

The girl and her family accepted the plea, Bertram said, because they did not want the ordeal of a trial.

While awaiting sentence, the man attempted to contract his daughters in violation of the court's instructions, Bertram said. He said bond was revoked and during the hearing, the man denied his guilt.

The plea agreement was voided, Bertram said, and soon after the prosecutor's office learned that there were many more offenses than originally known. He said the girl also became willing to testify so another indictment was returned.

During testimony Thursday morning, the man's daughter, who is now 15, testified that she was "playing Barbies" when her father first came into her bedroom when the rapes began in July of 1996.

"He picked me up and threw me on the bed. I was scared to tell anyone."

The girl said she was embarrassed and hesitant to talk about what happened.

Jim Maples, attorney for the man, objected numerous times to questioning by Commonwealth's Attorney Barry Bertram. He claimed the questions were leading.

George overruled the objections.

In his closing arguments, Maples argued that the testimony the jury heard was not the girl's but was Barry Bertram's.

"She didn't testify, Mr. Bertram did," Maples said. "She had to be led into almost every answer. She didn't know the story well enough to tell the story."

John Bertram in his closing arguments said his father

asked the questions he did only because the girl was reluctant to talk. The answers, he said, were clearly hers.

"He had to ask questions to help her, but the answers were hers," John Bertram said. "It was difficult for her. If these things happened, would you expect her to come in and rattle them off?"

The girl testified that her father had sexual intercourse with her "almost every weekend" and oral sex "every other time. He puts his mouth places where it shouldn't be."

She testified that she did not want to have sex and had asked her father many times to stop.

After almost three years, the girl testified, she feared she was pregnant and wrote a letter to her counselor. Her mother found the letter and that began the process that ultimately led to charges being filed against her father.

Maples in his closing arguments said the charges came about during a custody battle. He said his client was having trouble getting visitation rights.

"You have to be extremely skeptical," Maples told the jury.

A neighbor, who baby-sat for the girl and her sister, said she would have never believed that any of the charges were true.

"I would have trusted the lives of my kids with him," she said.

After allegations were made against the man, his neighbor said, he came for a visit.

"I told him he was going to have to get a lawyer or someone to help him out," the neighbor said. "He then said, 'I have something to tell you. You can't tell anyone and you probably will never want your children around me.' He said I would never want to be his friend again.

"'Everything that has been said about me, I have done.'

"I couldn't say nothing. I couldn't talk. I was so shocked. I still am to this day."

Kentucky State Police Detective Lisa Rudzinski testified that the man confessed to her.

The man testified Thursday that he admitted guilt only to "draw everyone out."

Maples said in his closing arguments that his client's actions were "stupid" but designed only to bring the matter to court so the truth could be brought out and he could regain visitation rights.

John Bertram suggested in his closing arguments that

the man may have been the best witness for the prosecution.

Bertram said the man didn't express disgust, disbelief or any similar emotion when asked how he felt to be accused of raping his daughter.

"He said it was bull crap."

During John Bertram's closing arguments, the accused said his neighbor's statements were a lie, "we ain't done yet."

Bertram said the man's outbursts did distract him, but helped make his case.

George on three occasions warned the man to keep quiet.

The only person who mentioned a custody dispute, John Bertram said, was the accused.

John Bertram called the neighbor one of the most credible witnesses he had ever heard. If the accused isn't lying, he said, then all of the other witnesses have to be and they have nothing to gain.

The accused's insistence that he pleaded guilty only to bring the matter to court and get at the truth, John Bertram said, doesn't make sense.

"Folks, it doesn't add up," John Bertram told the jury.

A look at the basics

Who

The man in the story is not identified to protect his daughter's identity. It's unusual for the major character of a story to not be identified. Others in the story include the judge, defense and prosecuting attorneys, a state police detective and the man's daughter.

What

The subject of the story is a shocking one – a man found guilty of repeatedly raping his daughter weekly for three years. The length of the sentence, 5,640 years, is also significant especially since it was believed to be the longest ever handed down in Kentucky. That *had* to be in the lead.

When

The length of sentence and the number of years the daughter was raped were all important time elements.

Where

The fact this happened in Taylor County made it quite significant. This wasn't a story about sexual abuse somewhere else. It happened at home. That disturbed many people.

Why

Why the man did what he did was not explained in court or in the story. One can only wonder as to the reasons for such acts.

How

The story explains how the abuse began and includes some of the daughter's testimony. That's necessary. This is a serious matter with serious consequences.

The story does not dwell on details of the abuse. That's probably best considering the subject matter.

Who cares

The entire community cared. Most were outraged to learn what this man was accused and found guilty of doing.

Sources

The story is based on attendance at the trial and some brief interviews after it was over. I was not present for all of the testimony. I was there for opening arguments, testimony of key witnesses and closing arguments. I was also present when the jury delivered its verdict.

Etc.

A trial such as this one isn't easy to cover. The subject matter should disturb anyone. It's a story, however, that has to be covered. Readers need to know what happens in their own community regardless of how disgusting it might be.

It's interesting to note that the man was granted a new trial months later. That trial was moved to Marion County where a jury found him not guilty.

Pay attention during trials. Take good notes. Ask questions of both the defense and prosecuting attorneys, if necessary, when court is not in session. Don't assume guilt or innocence. Present both sides of the case as equitable as possible.

Summarize as best as possible. There's no way to include everything. Be fair, though, in deciding what to include.

Explain something if it is not clear. For example, this man was sentenced to 5,640 years. He would have been eligible for parole in 12 years had he not been granted a new trial and ultimately found not guilty.

The prosecutor hoped that such a long sentence would influence a parole board's decision and keep the man in jail longer than 12 years. The story explains that. That information was not part of the trial. It came from questioning afterwards.

Think about what readers would want to know. Try to answer all questions.

This story, however, does not answer the question most people probably had: "Why would a father rape his daughter?"

I don't know if anyone can answer that.

Chapter 13
Special events

As a reporter, you might be called upon to cover a Miss America Pageant, a visit by the President of the United States or a movie company in town to film several scenes for a potential Oscar winning movie.

You may also cover something more routine such as a groundbreaking for a hospital expansion, a press conference to announce a new industry coming to town, a Relay for Life (a drive to raise money to fight cancer) or an Independence Day Celebration.

All types of special events can happen in your community. Covering them is a bit different than writing about meetings, court actions, typical features and most other stories.

First, they don't happen on a regular basis. You may or may not get some advance notice – most likely you will. Do as much research as possible about the event. Find out where and when things will happen. Know the sources to talk with before, during and after the event.

Special events may also last for a few minutes, a few hours or even a few days. That can affect coverage greatly.

Can you cover the entire event or just portions of it?

The event could also happen almost anywhere. If a local young woman, for example, wins the Miss Kentucky Pageant and then competes in the Miss America Pageant, you can't stay at home and cover it. Some traveling will be in order or you'll have to find a free-lancer to provide coverage.

Most likely you will want to be there yourself.

Every event is different. Find out all you can. Then decide the best way to cover it.

During my years as news editor for the Central Kentucky News-Journal, three young women from Campbellsville competed in the Miss America Pageant and one in the Miss USA Pageant. I covered all four.

The Miss America Pageant is in Atlantic City, N.J. The Miss USA Pageant moves each year. The pageant I covered was in South Padre Island, Texas.

I did all of the research I could before attending each pageant. Prior to the pageant, I talked with each of the young women. I got to know them and their families as much as possible.

That made it much easier to interview them when the actual pageant arrived.

It certainly was much easier to cover my third Miss America Pageant than my first. By then, I knew my way around Atlantic City to a certain extent. I knew where to get credentials, something about the convention center and how things worked.

Ask those involved pertinent questions. When can you take photos and where? When can you ask questions and where? What access do you have to the contestants and to the convention center?

Where will I sit during the pageant?

The contestants and their families can help with some of those questions. That can put you in touch with state pageant officials who can then put you in touch with the national officials.

Planning is the key.

Arrive early, if possible. That gives you time to get the "lay of the land" before the event begins. Also remember that you are interested in the young woman from your home town.

She's the reason you are at the pageant. Your stories must focus on her.

Let's look at a story from one of the Miss America Pageants I covered.

Veronica Duka makes Top 10 at Miss America

Only hours before the finals of the Miss America Pageant, Veronica Duka was wondering if she would be making a fleeting appearance on NBC or singing for the world.

Duka said her parents and grandparents were also sitting "on pins and needles" wondering if she would be in the Top 10.

She need not have worried.

The 19-year-old Campbellsville native was one of only 11 Miss Kentuckys to make the finals.

She's the first ever from Campbellsville to make the Top 10.

That put her on national television for the evening wear competition, the swimsuit competition and the talent competition.

If she hadn't made the Top 10, she would have appeared briefly on national television.

"Being named to the Top 10 was a relief," Duka said

Monday.

The pressure had been on until then, Duka said. She said making the finals allowed her "to just have fun."

The "best of the best" were in the Top 10, Duka said.

She was also the youngest of the finalists and one of the youngest in the pageant.

Most were 23 and 24.

Some of the girls have competed five years and more, Duka said. She's been involved in pageants for about two years.

Duka sang "Somewhere" to much applause from the audience in the Atlantic City Convention Center.

On Friday, Duka said the thought of performing on live television to millions of viewers all over the world "blows my mind."

"In itself it is a dream come true to be on national television," Duka said. "I've also wanted people to be able to turn on their television and have the opportunity to see my face."

Participating in the pageant, Duka said, has convinced her that she wants to pursue a career in show business.

It's also given her additional confidence.

"It has changed each and every one of our lives." Duka said of her and the other 49 contestants. "I have proven things to myself. You go away from here with a stronger sense of self."

Numerous media interviews each day were common for Duka who often found cameras thrust in her face as she was asked question after question.

"That doesn't faze me anymore," Duka said.

Duka used the media attention to promote her platform issue, multicultural education.

Many pageant observers thought her platform would attract the attention of the judges. There's a need to bring people of all cultures together, one observer said, and her platform could help do that.

Duka's father is white and her mother is black. She has said during many interviews that she considers being bi-racial an advantage.

Duka said she was amazed at how well all of the contestants got along and how easy it was to make friends.

"All the girls are sweet and cooperative," Duka said. "I've made many friends that I hope to keep in contact with."

Duka said she was surprised at how "cool and calm"

Veronica Duka sings during the talent portion of the Miss America Pageant.

she was. The first walk on the famous runway, though, was a bit emotional.

"We all walked out on the runway together the first time," Duka said. "We held hands and most of us were teary-eyed. It hit me where I was and what I was doing Tuesday night (during the first preliminary). That was pretty emotional."

Meeting the then-reigning Miss America, former Miss Americas, famous directors, dancers, choreographers and celebrities was exciting, Duka said.

Duka didn't make the Top Five. And the title ultimately went to Miss Kansas, Tara Dawn Holland.

"Winning is insignificant," Duka said. "It is an honor and a privilege to be here."

Duka said she knew she did her best and would be pleased whatever the outcome might be.

"Only one of us is going to leave here as Miss America," Duka said. "You have to take the experience and savor it for all it's worth. You have to have fun and make all the friends you can. You need to enjoy it all you can and savor the experience."

Duka said she plans to concentrate now on being Miss Kentucky.

She returned home Monday for a brief visit.

"I just wanted to be with friends and family for awhile and to relax," Duka said.

The remainder of the week is full of public appearances.

Duka said she will be home for the Miss Campbellsville Pageant in November. She also hopes to attend some football games and perhaps sing the "National Anthem."

Duka said she knows she's a better person after competing in the Miss American Pageant.

She's also weighing her options.

A look at the basics
Who

Veronica Duka is the subject of the story.

What

Duka's appearance in the Miss America Pageant was the focus of the story. How she placed and her experiences are key to the story.

When

The story was timely. By that, the story had to appear in print as soon after the pageant as possible.

Because the Central Kentucky News-Journal is published twice each week, it was possible to have coverage of preliminary competitions in the Thursday issue prior to the Saturday night competition.

Where

The pageant may have happened in Atlantic City, N.J., but it was still very much a local story.

Why

The story details Duka's experiences and also touches on why she decided to seek the Miss America crown.

How

Hard work, talent, experience, maturity and many other factors are involved in a Miss America Pageant. The story talks about that. It also talks about how Duka was changed by the pageant and what it might mean to her future.

Who cares

Duka was of great interest to the entire community and to many residents of Kentucky. She was one of 11 from Kentucky to ever make the Top 10 and the first from Campbellsville. A local girl from a small town competing for Miss America is a major story.

Sources

Duka was the primary source. I was able to talk with her several times during the week of the pageant. Pageant officials also provided needed information. My own observations also were part of this story and others written about the pageant.

Etc.

Communication has improved since my coverage of Miss America and Miss USA. While I took a notebook computer with me for each of the pageants, I had to mail floppy discs with my stories to the newspaper prior to my return home. E-mail communication was unrealistic at the time.

In addition to writing a variety of stories, I also took photographs. Digital cameras at the time were virtually non-existent. Film I shot early in the week at most of the pageants was sent back to the newspaper by Fed-Ex. Today, it would be easy to take digital photos of the competitions, edit them on a notebook computer and send them as well as the stories by e-mail.

At major events, don't become overwhelmed.

There were celebrities everywhere and major media including

large newspapers, magazines and television networks.

Don't let any of that distract you from your task. Complete your assignment.

Welcome, Mr. President

It's not everyday that a President of the United States comes to your community or within a few miles of it.

When Jimmy Carter came to Bardstown in August 1979, it was a major story. Obviously, state media and the media in Bardstown (Nelson County) devoted many inches to the visit.

Shelbyville is about an hour's drive from Bardstown. Nevertheless, the editor and publisher of The Sentinel-News believed the story was one worth covering.

I was sent to write the story and take photos of the visit.

In the back of my mind was the need for a local angle, a Shelbyville angle. I was able to find one as you'll discover from the story.

Some preparation was needed.

Press credentials were necessary to take photos from vantage points that would guarantee good photos.

Without such credentials, reporters would have to mingle with the crowd and jockey for the best viewing positions.

Press credentials also permitted reporters and photographers to ride in a vehicle in front of the presidential motorcade or walk along the parade route.

Credentials also were needed to cover the scheduled town meeting.

I can't recall how the press credentials were obtained.

I know that a request had to be submitted and authorities made a background check. They must have determined I wasn't a lunatic and posed no threat.

My credentials were issued.

If you are in doubt as to who the contact people are for such events as visits by a President, check with your state's press association. Someone with the association should be able to help.

The Kentucky Press Association, for example, is an invaluable source of information.

Carter receives warm welcome

Jimmy Carter got out of his car in Bardstown Tuesday and mingled with the thousands who came to see him. It was hard to believe this was the president many have lost confidence in.

The entire town warmed to Carter and most of the people lining the route of the motorcade wore Carter buttons sold by the Bardstown Chamber of Commerce. There were also many signs welcoming the president and one said simply "Jimmy, we love you."

At least one family from Shelbyville managed to get a glimpse of the president. Hugh Leachman and his family were on their way home from a trip to Mammoth Cave. They took a detour hoping to see Carter and they weren't disappointed.

Carter was late which caused many Bardstown residents to wonder if he was going to show. The delay was apparently caused by a thunderstorm that threatened the town at about 3 p.m., only minutes before the scheduled arrival of the president.

Marine One, the helicopter that brought the president to Bardstown from Louisville, reportedly didn't want to be in the air while it was lightning.

The delay gave Leachman time to pick a spot along the route of the motorcade from which his family could watch.

"He just zipped through," Leachman said. "We could see him smiling through the window."

The president arrived at the Nelson County Courthouse at approximately 4:53 p.m. The motorcade then turned down Third Street. The presidential limousine stopped and Carter got out. But many people couldn't see him because of the crowd.

Carter jumped on top of his car and stayed there for several blocks. State troopers lined the streets, preventing the crowd from getting too close. Secret service agents flanked the car.

Near the end of the motorcade, Carter got back in his car for the short trip to Bardstown High School where he met 2,000 citizens. They represented several counties and each had tickets given out last week. For many, obtaining those tickets had meant a long wait and most arrived at the high school around noon to secure a good seat.

Carter arrived at the high school at approximately 5:10 p.m., 25 minutes later than scheduled. Because of the delay, he didn't meet with staff as planned and went directly to the town meeting.

Appropriately, "My Old Kentucky Home" was sung and then "Hail to the Chief." Carter was introduced by Gus Wilson, mayor of Bardstown.

Leachman didn't have tickets to the town meeting. So he and his family listened to radio coverage as they drove home.

"I think he sold the people," Leachman said, "plus it didn't hurt John Y. Brown's cause at all."

Brown, the democratic nominee for governor, accompanied Carter along with Governor Julian Carroll, Senator Wendell Ford, and Senator Walter D. Huddleston. Brown's wife, Phyllis George Brown, was also present.

Carter spoke for a few minutes before fielding 14 questions. The need for conservation was emphasized after he apologized for not visiting earlier. The president seemed at home in the small town of about 7,000.

The first question Carter was asked concerned the rising number of illegitimate births and the condition of this country's welfare system.

"One of the most important things we need to do is strengthen the American family," Carter said. He also commented on the role religion needs to play in the nation.

The next question was asked by a young boy, but the microphone didn't work. Carter won over the crowd when he invited the youngster to share his microphone.

Carter was asked other questions ranging from telephone service in Bullitt County to Salt II negotiations.

The town meeting lasted an hour. For many, that proved almost unbearable for the temperature in the high school gym was soaring in the nineties.

Most people were pleased with Carter's appearance and his answers to the questions.

"I'm a Carter fan," said one woman carrying a fan obtained from a local church.

Most people were smiling and happy. They obviously love Jimmy.

A look at the basics
Who
While the story is primarily about President Jimmy Carter, it also mentions Hugh Leachman. Leachman was from Shelby County. That provided a needed local tie to the visit.

What
The subject, of course, is a visit by the president and how he was received.

When
Any visit of a president is significant. The timing of this one was important. Carter's popularity had declined in recent months. His wife had been in Bardstown a few months earlier and left after a brief visit because of illness.

Residents needed a reason to feel good about the president. This visit gave them a reason.

Where
The visit was to Bardstown, an hour's drive from Shelbyville.

Why
As previously mentioned, Carter was in Bardstown to regain some popularity and to make up for a visit his wife had to cut short.

How
The story provides some details about security during a presidential visit. It also tells how Carter came across to the crowd and how the crowd responded.

Who cares
Who could miss a chance to see a president? Few, I would wager. A presidential visit is rare. Luckily I was able to find at least one Shelbyville resident who saw Carter and included his comments in the story. That helped localize it and make it more relevant to the readers of The Sentinel-News.

Sources

Though I didn't speak directly to Carter, his comments during the town meeting were included. Leachman was my primary source, if you're only counting people I spoke to personally. My observations are also included.

Etc.

I spent most of the day in Bardstown waiting for the president and following him as he made his way around town. There were dozens of other reporters from all over the state.

All wanted the best vantage point for photos. I had to do my best to make certain I had a clear view of Carter. In a similar situation, you may have to force your wait to the front or at least make certain no one else pushes you out of the way. You don't want to be part of the herd – you want to be at the front of it.

There are some statements in my story that I wouldn't include if I were writing it today. Those are statements that as an editor I would not permit.

I'm talking about personal opinion.

Observations are one matter. Opinions are another.

How could I have possibly determined from observations alone that those who gathered to see Carter had confidence in his ability as president? Also, look at the last line of the story, "They obviously love Jimmy."

If a reporter turned in a story with such a statement for me to edit, I would have one simple question.

"Says who?"

Perhaps all of those statements would have been OK had an editor's note said: "This story contains the observations and conclusions of the writer."

Those statements certainly should not be in a "straight" news story. Do you remember the line from the television show "Dragnet" that Joe Friday made popular?

"Just the facts ma'am, just the facts."

There's another problem with the story. Marine One doesn't want to be in the air when it's lightning? Marine One is a helicopter. It's capable of independent thought?

I think not.

Those in charge of Marine One might not have wanted to fly in a thunderstorm. Certainly, the helicopter could not have decided that for itself.

Lights, camera, action

It was a big deal in Shelby County when 20th Century Fox came to town. The movie company brought with it some major stars and a major director.

As you can imagine, all of that attracted much attention. The movie set, however, was closed to all but those involved. A few telephone calls resulted in permission to visit the set and talk with those involved.

That was largely possible because of the people who owned the farm where filming was taking place. They were open to publicity and made the newspaper aware of what was happening long before the stars came out.

The family provided the contacts necessary for permission to be present while filming was under way.

Movie stars in Finchville

20th Century Fox comes to county

Margot Kidder munched on an apple as she emerged from the rear of the farmhouse at Finchville.

She joined the rest of the cast and crew of "Willie and Phil" who were gathered around the camera where director Paul Mazursky was giving instructions. A make-up girl carefully adjusted Ms. Kidder's costume in preparation for a run-through of one scene.

Kidder is best known for her role as Lois Lane in "Superman." She also stars in "The Amityville Horror" which opened recently in Louisville.

The actors ran through their lines and made the moves that will eventually be visible on the screen. Mazursky obviously liked what he saw. The sun was being cantankerous and threatening to go behind a cloud so he decided to try for a take.

Watching all the action from under a nearby shade tree were Jim and Linda Weixler, owners of the farmhouse, and their daughters Kathleen and Stephanie. It was Tuesday, the first day of shooting and already the Weixlers had become friends with the cast and crew.

Weixler said he probably took over 200 photos of the

stars Tuesday morning. And the family got to eat lunch with the cast.

Mr. and Mrs. John Tully, who owned the farmhouse when it was first scouted, were also watching the filming. Their horses and furniture will be used in several scenes.

"Everything's really been going great," said Terry Donnelly, production manager for the film, which is being made by Twentieth Century Fox. He said the local people have really been friendly and very cooperative.

"Willie and Phil" is a contemporary story about two men in love with the same woman, according to Mazursky. The scene at the farmhouse details a visit Willie takes with Jeanette to visit her mother in Kentucky.

Michael Ontkean, who plays Willie, and Kidder, who plays Jeanette, spent most of Tuesday morning in a Volkswagen filming scenes of their arrival at the farm.

Mazursky chose Kentucky for the scene partially for sentimental reasons. His wife Betsy was born in Louisville and her aunt, who was 101, lived in Russellville until she died this July 3. The director had planned a party for her.

In 1954, Mazursky come to Kentucky for the first time with his wife in a Volkswagen. That trip planted the seed for the scene.

In May, Kidder said, she came to Shelby County with Mazursky looking for a site for the movie. Several had been chosen by the Kentucky Film Commission.

"We drove all over the county, Kidder said. "It's beautiful. It's very much like Quebec where I grew up."

Kidder said she has a photo taken of herself at age four on the front porch of a house identical to the one in Finchville. She has spent her spare time getting to know local residents watching the filming.

Though the filming was scheduled over three days, Donnelly said, only about six minutes of the movie will take place in Finchville. Mazursky said other scenes will be in New York, California, Hawaii, and India. The movie is scheduled to be released in January.

The filming has attracted a lot of attention in Finchville but crowds have been kept to a minimum by state police. Weixler said about 20 of his neighbors and friends did drop by Tuesday. He said he tried to keep it "hush" so the crowd would be as small as possible.

Weixler said he was amazed at the attention to detail there is in making a movie. The scene of Willie and Jeanette arriving required three takes before Mazursky was satisfied.

The house, which is about 125 years old, was chosen for the movie because of the vista from the road leading to it, according to Mazursky. He also said the size and proximity of the tobacco barn is important because Jeanette and Willie walk to it from the house in one scene.

Donnelly said the movie has a budget of almost $6 million. That's average for this type of film, he said, since costs are steadily going up largely because of labor.

Mazursky is also a star. He has directed and written such films as "Bob & Carol & Ted & Alice," "Next Stop Greenwich Village," "Blume In Love," "Alex In Wonderland," "Harry and Tonto" and "An Unmarried Woman."

Weixler said all of the cast and crew, despite their fame, have been really nice. "They're super people," he said. No pun intended.

A look at the basics
Who
The subject is the filming of a movie, "Willie and Phil." The who consists of the stars, the director and the owners of the property in Finchville where about six minutes of the movie was filmed.

What
The story focuses on what brought the movie company to town. It also focuses on what's involved in completing six minutes of a movie.

When
Three days in Finchville was the time allotted for the movie. The filming took place in summer of 1979. The movie was released in 1980. Because of the shooting schedule, the filming concluded on the day the story was published.

Where
Filming took place in Finchville, only a few miles outside Shelbyville, in Shelby County. It was a local story that also attracted the attention of the Louisville Courier-Journal. The Courier-Journal had the story first only because it is a daily newspaper.

Why

The story answers why Finchville was selected. The farmhouse chosen had the "right" look as determined by Kidder and Mazursky.

How

A glimpse of how movies are made and what stars are really like is part of the story.

Who cares

The movie "Superman" was still fresh on most people's minds when Kidder came to town. She was a major star at the time. And, what community won't be interested in knowing that scenes for a major motion picture were being filmed in their backyards?

Sources

There were many sources for the story. The former and current owners of the property provided valuable information and contacts. The production manager, Kidder, Ontkean and Mazursky all took time to talk about their jobs and their impressions of Shelby County.

Etc.

Talking with movie stars is fun. Kidder was wonderful. She really was. She put me at ease and talked with me as if we were old friends.

Mazursky was a bit different. He was wearing a University of Kentucky cap when I met him. I thought I would break the ice by asking if he were a UK fan.

"Somebody just gave me this cap," he said.

No ice was broken. If anything, the temperature dropped. I did manage, however, to get enough information from Mazursky for the story.

Stories such as this one can help a reporter forget about some of those that are not so pleasant to do. Being a reporter can be fun.

Chapter 14
Enjoy your job

Even in a small town, being a reporter could mean rubbing elbows with celebrities, talking with the governor or flying around the country in military helicopters.

Enjoy such things.

Being a reporter should be fun. If it's not, you're probably going to be buying antacids by the case. I once had a boss who kept a large bottle of a famous, over-the-counter antacid in his desk and on occasion would reach for it and take a large gulp.

He even offered me a taste once. I passed.

Have as much fun on the job as possible. If you don't, you most surely will suffer at times. Being a reporter and/or editor can be stressful. As I've already said, it's possible to have both a great day and a really horrible day all on the same day.

That's the nature of the business. And that's probably because you deal with people.

Over the years, I have been fortunate. Indeed, I have been blessed. I have met and written about some really great people. Some of them have been notable folks that not everyone would have a chance to meet or talk with let alone get paid to do so.

I've also met some folks that Will Rogers never met. (Rogers was a humorist who boasted that he never met a man he didn't like.)

There are rude, arrogant people out there. There are mean people out there. There are people who lie, cheat, steal and do other not-so-nice things. You will meet some of them. Forget them if you can.

You will work long hours. You will make mistakes. There will be stories that embarrass and otherwise hurt people. You will see things that will turn your stomach. You will become disillusioned. People will fuss and complain. Many will never thank you no matter how good a story is.

Remember the people who do compliment you. On occasion, write about something that interests you. Remember the good stuff.

Enjoy watching history happen.

Only a few weeks into my first job as a reporter for the Sturgis News in Sturgis, Ky. I was asked to accompany the local high school band to Evansville, Ind. for a visit by President Gerald Ford. The ride wasn't exactly memorable, but finding a place along the main thoroughfare of the city for photos of both the band and the President was.

I grew up in a small town and had virtually been nowhere in my life. I might have seen a mayor or county judge, but never a PRESIDENT.

On the tops of buildings everywhere I looked were men in suits. Many had guns. All had earpieces, concealed as much as possible.

After waiting what seemed like hours, I saw the presidential limousine and in the back was Gerald Ford.

I remember thinking that he looked in person just like he did on TV. Remember, I was only 20 or so and very impressionable.

I almost met my first governor that year.

Gov. Julian Carroll was scheduled to be at a luncheon in Sturgis for local officials, a few select dignitaries and the media. I wasn't the only reporter at the newspaper but for some reason I was assigned to cover his visit.

I recall interviewing a hog farmer that morning and changing clothes before the luncheon. If you've ever been around a hog farm, you should understand the need for fresh clothing before meeting a governor.

For some reason I didn't take a fresh pair of shoes with me to work that day. I should have. I'll leave an explanation of that statement up to your imagination.

The luncheon must have been uneventful because I don't remember anything else about it.

About three years later, I found myself in Bardstown, Ky. covering a visit by President Jimmy Carter as mentioned previously. This time I had press passes issued by the White House and Secret Service.

I was also able to get much closer to Carter than I had to Ford.

About the same time, I also covered the filming of "Willie and Phil" as discussed in the last chapter.

Kidder was friendly. I sat on a stool next to her and discussed such things as how friendly the people in the area were and how good the food was.

Mazursky wasn't the friendliest person in the world as I have already mentioned.

I was present when Woody Harrelson came to Campbellsville for the grand opening of the Kentucky Hemp Museum. That's right, a museum dedicated to hemp, once existed in Taylor County.

Harrelson, who played Woody on the TV sitcom "Cheers" and

Woody Harrelson was joined by Donna Cockrel for the opening of the Kentucky Hemp Museum. Cockrel, was a Simpsonville Elementary School teacher, who came under fire for her position on industrial hemp.

starred in such movies as "Natural Born Killers," visited several counties in Kentucky promoting agricultural hemp. He was arrested elsewhere for planting hemp seeds.

There was an attempt several years ago to bring hemp back as an agricultural crop, perhaps to replace tobacco. Mind you, I'm talking about the kind of hemp that doesn't produce the high associated with marijuana.

Kentucky farmers decades ago grew hemp for rope and other byproducts. The Kentucky Hemp Museum sold legal products made from hemp.

Woody Harrelson reads the story I wrote about his pending visit. Is this shameful self-promotion or an ideal way to cover a story?
How much coverage does a visit by Harrelson deserve?
Hint, he was a major TV and movie star. How often does someone like that visit a relatively small town?

Hundreds of people crowded into the small museum to meet Harrelson and secure an autograph. It was quite a scene. They all seemed to love him. Many asked me to get photos of them with Harrelson.

It was impossible, of course, to honor all the requests.

Harrelson was fascinated by a story I had written about the prospects for agricultural hemp. I managed to get a photo of him reading that story.

While I wouldn't equate Harrelson's visit with that of a president, writing about him, photographing him and talking with him was memorable. He was one of the more interesting characters I have met.

Then again, I have many pleasant memories from my years as a practicing journalist.

The following column sums up my newspaper career and mentions many of the more memorable events during my 26 years in the business.

There are many 'big stories' when you are a reporter

Someone a few weeks ago, after learning I would soon be changing careers, asked me what the "biggest" story I've ever covered was.

I couldn't come up with an answer.

Friday was my last day as news editor of the Central Kentucky News-Journal. I'm now an assistant professor of journalism at Campbellsville University.

I still don't know what I would consider as my "biggest" story.

Over the last 21 years in Campbellsville, three years in Shelbyville and two years in Sturgis, I've covered stories of all kinds.

I've photographed two presidents and numerous movie stars. I've also photographed three Miss America pageants and the Miss USA pageant. I've been to France and wrote about a town there that was to be Campbellsville's sister city.

I've been to Frankfort. I've been to Washington, D.C. I've talked with governors, senators, congressmen and the like.

Once I stood next to U.S. Senator Wendell Ford in a men's room.

I've touched the names of young men from Taylor County who are enshrined on the Vietnam Memorial. I have touched a simple cross which marks the grave of a Taylor Countian buried in a cemetery overlooking the beaches at Normandy.

I've talked with the families of those young men.

I've attended numerous Memorial Day and Veterans Day ceremonies. I've photographed the raising of the flags, the placement of flowers on the Taylor County War Memorial and salutes honoring our fallen heroes.

Without joining the military, I've flown on transport planes and helicopters to military bases in three states. I've gone for rides in tanks and missile launchers.

I've eaten field rations, snails and ostrich burgers.

I've seen marijuana. I've seen shirts and belts made of hemp.

My image, complete with camera, is included in Fred Thrasher's 1991 print of Campbellsville's Fourth of July Celebration.

I've been in Freedom Hall and watched and photographed a high school team claim a state championship. I also watched a high school coach and her basketball team play their hearts out and the season end with a heartbreaker.

I've photographed a college team playing in the national championships.

I've photographed local bands competing in the state finals both at Commonwealth Stadium and at Western Kentucky University.

I've been to the auctions at Keeneland. I once rode an elephant.

Over the years, I've flown numerous times in big planes, small planes, and hot air balloons.

I'm scared of heights.

I rode the rails between Lebanon and Campbellsville in a passenger car pulled by a steam engine.

I've been on numerous boats all over Green River Lake. I sat, briefly, on the hot seat in a dunk tank.

I can't swim.

I've photographed tractors, farmers, beauty contestants, seasoned soldiers in khaki uniforms, fatal accidents, minor accidents, fires, youngsters returning to school, celebrations, bands dressed in Civil War uniforms, the firing of cannon balls, sporting events, dead snakes, strange vegetables, trials and buildings under construction.

I've photographed an eye surgeon operating on a horse.

I've written about factory closings and industrial announcements. I've written about drunk drivers, Social Security and the need for all of us to get along.

I've written stories about people suffering from cancer and other diseases. I've talked with parents and spouses who have lost loved ones to disease, poorly constructed roads and drunk drivers.

I've written about KY 210 and taken photos of improvements that were long overdue. I've also written about plans for a lodge at Green River Lake.

I've seen murderers, sex offenders, child molesters and drug dealers.

I've written about missionaries, agencies offering a helping hand and a man who was led to buy a deserted church and repair it so it could once more serve the Lord.

I've learned about car restoration, model airplanes, antiques, water gardening, roses, flowers, baseball cards, coin collecting, magic and an assortment of other hobbies and interests.

Over the years, I've attended close to 300 fiscal court meetings and a like number of school board meetings. I've been to numerous city council meetings, zoning board meetings, press conferences, ground breakings, dinners of all kinds, elections, debates and more.

I've written about test scores for our school children, dress codes, computer systems that can monitor classroom behavior, a child who was left on a bus, vacancies on school boards and a variety of educational issues.

I've kept up with the problems facing tobacco farmers. I followed a tobacco farmer through an entire season.

I've written about droughts and corn crops. I've written about a man who made extra money by raising and selling vegetables.

I've praised politicians in columns and also offered criticism.

I watched as our neighbors went off to war. I was there when one after returning from war renewed his wedding vows.

I've been in many people's homes, yards, gardens, businesses and churches.

I've shared people's pain and their hopes and joys.

They were all big stories to someone. And I just realized how much they all meant to me.

A look at the basics
Who

This column is very personal. It sums up my career as a journalist. While I am the who in this column, I would like to think it also is representative of other journalists.

What

The column is about my experiences as a journalist, the good times and the not so good times.

When

The column covers 26 years. It was written at the end of one career and the beginning of another.

Why

I intended for the column to share what I consider to be some of the most significant stories I have covered. Most might not be Pulitzer Prize material, but all are about people for whom I genuinely cared.

How

The how is the effects the stories have had on me and shaped me as a member of the community.

Who cares

I certainly care. And judging from the reaction the column received, many in the community also cared. I also hope that those who were the subjects of the stories cared.

Etc.

This column was difficult to write. After completing it and reading it one last time, I realized the change I was making in my life. The fact I was no longer going to be a reporter hit home. That made me realize how fortunate I have been and how appreciative I am of all the wonderful people I have met.

Writing this also makes me pause and reflect for a moment.

Being a reporter can indeed be one of the best jobs in the world.

Chapter 15
A writer must write

A few of the best writers I have known over the last several years never went to college. They liked people, weren't afraid to ask questions and wrote almost constantly.

They worked relentlessly to become better reporters and writers. All wished they had university degrees. They probably could have been even better at what they did had they gone to college.

A college education is important. But it alone won't make anyone a good reporter, photographer or editor. You can only master something by doing it. That might not qualify as an epiphany. Then again, it might.

Most universities today require an internship as part of their curriculum for journalism, public relations or any other form of mass communication.

As an editor I would hire someone with a college degree *and* experience of any kind over someone with a degree who had never written a thing. The point is – a writer must write. Reporters must also report and editors also must edit.

In the same vein, a photographer must photograph.

Would you trust your life to a surgeon who had completed all medical coursework but had never actually performed a surgery? I don't think so.

There are stories everywhere just waiting to be written.

Most newspapers, radio stations, television stations and the like gladly will work with aspiring journalists. As a professor, I have helped students obtain experience with a local newspaper, radio station, chamber of commerce, industrial recruiter's office, hospital, mayor's office, judge's office and the public relations office on campus.

The majority of these part-time positions didn't pay a thing. They were, however, immensely invaluable for those who put some energy into them.

Ask those who work for such businesses if they would mind you spending a few days looking over their shoulders. Ask if you could write something and submit it for possible publication or broadcast.

More and more classes today are being designed with writing for real businesses in mind.

That, in my opinion, is essential.

You must have clips to show prospective employers when you graduate and begin looking for a job in the "real" world.

Look for interesting stories. They are all around us.

What's the most unusual patient your eye doctor has ever treated? I once did a story about an ophthalmologist who worked with a veterinarian to remove a horse's cataract. It was a fascinating story.

How about the family who lives just down the street that came to this country from Laos? Two former students at Campbellsville University (Campbellsville College at the time) had to flee Laos in the aftermath of Vietnam.

Their stories spoke volumes about the horrors of war.

If you saw a man on Main Street driving an old car with no roof and a mule sitting in the back seat, would you notice? Could you write an interesting story about why that mule is riding around town?

How do you even get the mule in the car?

(There was a man in Campbellsville several years ago who did take his mule for rides in his car.)

Would a story about a man who for decades has raised tomatoes and peppers to sell from the hood of his car at a local shopping center be of interest?

Could you accompany a trucker on a long-distance run and write a story about what it's like to spend much of your life on the road?

How many people die each year so poor that the county has to pay their burial expenses? You might be surprised. Such a story can be revealing and heart wrenching.

What's it like to be a police officer, firefighter, security guard, grocery clerk or work the front counter at a busy fast food restaurant? Those people all have good stories to tell.

Talk with these people. Sharpen your interviewing skills. Polish your writing. Get published.

I'm willing to wager that a good writer can walk across a typical university campus, go for a stroll in any neighborhood or take a short drive around town and come up with a story idea.

As I've already said, story ideas are everywhere. Look for them, find them and write them.

Write them even if no one has asked you to do so. Ask your professors to review those stories. Once you have gotten them right, put them in your portfolio.

I want to share a story written by my daughter, Calen, as a university freshman in the spring of 2002. I sent it, without a byline, to the

Central Kentucky News-Journal where it was reviewed by the editor, publisher and a staff writer. They liked what they saw.

And when a part-time position as a writer became available, my daughter was asked to interview. She did, and she was hired.

While I will admit that I'm not completely objective when looking at her work, I truly believe it is among the best newspaper writing I have ever seen from a freshman.

She also took the photo that accompanies the story.

A DawnBreaker

With a flip of a switch the curling irons and hair come to life and begin to warm. A sweep of the floor and chairs is all that is needed to prepare for the day.

The smocks are washed, the towels are ready, the scissors are cleaned and this hairdresser is waiting for the day to begin.

Jackie Pierce works as a hairdresser.

Jackie, owner of Jackie's Hair and Nails, has short blond hair, with a hint of honey highlights, which often changes color and style due to her profession. She is a joy to be around and is very much a "people" person.

Jackie will brighten your mood and uplift your spirits.

She wears a cotton shirt or pantsuit, along with her smock, with her comfortable tennis shoes that allow her to be on her feet all day. You will never see her without a smile on her face and never talk to her without hearing her laugh.

Jackie has a gentle way about her when it comes to her clients, and she is very talkative. She has no gray hair, which could be because she knows how to get rid of it. She is 57 years old, but you would never be able to tell.

A customer walks into the shop and is greeted with "Hey darlin'. How ya doin'?"

You can hear the sound of a soap opera on a well-worn television, hair dryers humming and gossip in the background. Those tiny hairs you never seem to get rid of are everywhere and the faint smell of hairspray begins to grow on those stopping by for the latest 'do.

Dozens of shampoo and hair dye bottles and a rainbow of nail polish all sit on their shelves in the small and a bit cramped shop.

Two shampooing stations and four dryers are used daily and seem to be a bit worn. Home, fashion and "women" magazines are all over the shop, with their pages worn; coffee and Cokes are in the refrigerator, stools are scattered to put your feet on, and Jackie is there to go out of her way to make you comfortable.

A haircut costs you from $7 to $10 and some information about how the family is doing.

Jackie is always interested in what is going on and knowing anything exciting that has happened to you lately. She will do her best to fit you in because "People can't wait for a haircut," she said.

Jackie has an amazing ability to multi-task. She can cut your hair, carry on a conversation and answer the phone all at once. She is now using a headset to answer her many phone calls while never missing a snip. When she trims youngsters' hair she tells them to be really still so she won't have to add anything to her "jar of ears."

She said, "They always straighten up when I get to their ears; they're scared of me then."

Jackie has worked at her shop for 17 years, and doesn't plan on leaving.

Jackie was born in Lincoln County in 1945. She has made Campbellsville her home for 40 years and has been married to her husband, Johnie, for 39 years. She is the mother of two, a son and a daughter, and has three grandchildren.

Jackie wanted to go to college at the age of 39 but needed a job. She was touring with her husband's rock and roll band playing rhythm guitar. There were four members and were called the DawnBreakers.

This name was born during a long ride home from a show in Bowling Green. Jackie and Johnie were driving in the van and entered Campbellsville just as the dawn was breaking.

The name stuck.

They played Elvis tunes and cut five records. Before joining the band, Jackie made their costumes and attended every practice. This was an early sign of her dedication and caring for her family and friends.

One member then left and she was clearly the one to fill his shoes. She was then the rhythm guitar player. At a point in her life she decided that the band life was not the life she wanted anymore, so she left the band to become a hairdresser.

She had always done her family's hair, and she decided that would be a good job. She enrolled in the State Beauty

College in Campbellsville in 1985, and she completed her training in one year. She missed the band, but knew that she needed to have a steady career.

In January of 1991 the owner of the shop she had been working in, Associate of Hair Design, decided to leave. Jackie was settled in Campbellsville and did not want to move. She took over the shop and coined it Jackie's Hair and Nails.

She had always wanted to be a hairdresser, and never wants to change fields.

"I love it."

She loves coming to work. Every day is different, and she loves the excitement of not being able to predict what will happen. Nothing makes her happier than a person being truly happy with what she has done with their hair.

Jackie's workweek starts out right – with a day off. She works Tuesday through Friday and is fortunate enough to make her own hours. You can find her at home some days as early as 2 p.m., but sometimes not until 8 p.m.

Jackie will stay late to do your hair, and will schedule your appointment around your schedule. She does a little bit of everything. She does nails, hair, eyebrows, makeup, plus giving a little advice on your problems or her words of wisdom.

Proms, weddings, class nights, special occasions, some funerals, and everyday haircuts are her specialties. She absolutely loves doing acrylic nails, and recently got rid of what she hated most – pedicures.

Her clients range from tiny tots to elderly men and women, and she will never turn away a walk-in.

Her client relationship is something she values, and puts a lot of time into maintaining. On a recent afternoon she was cutting an elderly woman's hair. The woman, Ada Milby, has been going to Jackie for almost six years and is not about to go anywhere else.

Ada calls Jackie her "miracle maker" for performing magic on her "horrendous" hair. Ada says that Jackie always makes her feel comfortable by giving her coffee, putting her feet up, and helping her walk around. She says Jackie calls her "sexy" and "gorgeous"; that makes her feel good.

"When I make an appointment, Jackie asks me when can I be here, and she doesn't tell me a time she can fit me in. She makes me feel special and important," Ada says cheerfully.

Jackie Pierce prepares a customer's hair for a perm.

Jackie just keeps cutting with a smile on her face.

Jackie enjoys the spare time that she does get. She is a very busy woman, but she always makes some time to enjoy herself. She enjoys crafts, sewing, dressing as a clown at various local events, landscaping, cake decorating and reading.

"I try to learn everything," she said.

Overall, her favorite weekend activity is being with her grandchildren. She cherishes them and loves making them balloon animals and making them laugh. She was once active in the Society for the Prevention of Cruelty to Animals. She gave that up because she did not like begging for money for a very worthy cause.

She has a soft spot in her heart for people, and it truly shows when you spend time with her.

Ada is a regular client that visits Jackie once every two weeks. Ada paid her $8, and got a hug, and a young girl was next.

She only waited about 10 minutes and greeted Jackie warmly. Jackie said, "We shavin' it all off?"

That is usually the greeting she gives to all youngsters. They all laugh and secretly hope she is kidding.

The girl gets a haircut and gets her eyebrows waxed. Hot oil is poured on her, and Jackie ever-so-carefully pulls off the wax.

The girl winced in pain, and Jackie immediately put a towel on her to stop the burning pain. She is finished and borrows Jackie's phone to call her mom.

Her last client of the day is her eight-year-old nephew. He is getting rid of his "Harry Potter" haircut she gave him last time.

He says the girls like his hair too much, and he doesn't like that. So, Jackie goes to work. She buzzes his head and spikes up the front creating him a new identity.

Those girls won't know what hit them.

This story takes the reader to the beauty shop. It's easy to visualize exactly what the shop looks like, the customers and even Jackie.

It makes excellent use of quotes and provides the reader with a "slice of life" that's familiar to most. The reader can see the interaction between Jackie and her customers.

Some of the sentences, I believe, are really quite revealing and an experienced writer might not have come up with them.

This sentence, for example, is most illuminating and helps set the tone for the story: "She has no gray hair, which could be because she knows how to get rid of it."

Who could read that about a hairdresser and not smile at least just a little?

The story ends with the last customer of the day. He just happens to be Jackie's eight-year-old nephew who wants something different because the girls like his Harry Potter haircut way too much. A buzz cut seems to be ideal.

"Those girls won't know what hit them."

I love it. Reading the story should make most readers smile and feel good. Any feature that can do that is worth reading.

This particular story was written for an English composition class and does not follow journalistic style. Some editing would be necessary for publication in a newspaper.

There is some editorializing in the story. That, however, can easily be removed with a little careful editing. That aside, the story is wonderfully crafted and demonstrates an ability to capture detail and make a story come alive.

Listen, observe. Take notes. Read the work of others. But most of all – write.

Chapter 16
Your turn, identify the basic elements of these stories

One of the first feature stories I ever wrote was about a man in Morganfield, Ky. who raises buffalo. It had long been his dream to own some of the massive animals, possibly ride them and breed them with cattle.

While the story apparently was good enough to win a second-place award from the Kentucky Press Association, there are a couple of things about it that I don't like.

There are some changes I would make if I had the story to write all over again.

What do you think they are?

(I'll tell you in Appendix B what I don't like about the story.)

Could it have won a first-place award if the changes had been made?

Also, as you read the story, think about the who, what, when, where, why and how. Identify who would care about the story. The source should be easy to identify.

Hopefully at this point you can identify the problems with the story and the basics that make up its structure.

Would You Believe... Buffalo In Union County?

Motorists traveling on the St. Vincent road often pass the home of Donald Baird, slow down, and eagerly search for a place to turn around.

Heads begin popping out of windows.

"Is that a buffalo?" they gasp.

For Don Baird the answer is always "yes." Baird owns three head of buffalo – two bulls and a cow – which roam over his 148-acre farm.

For years Baird dreamed of owning a buffalo. He hoped to train it and eventually be able to ride it. In the back of his mind was also the idea of crossing buffalo with cattle. A couple of years ago Baird saw one of the only trained buffalo in existence at a rodeo in Missouri. The buffalo allowed his owner to ride him and would lie down on command.

That did it. Don Baird began searching for a seller of buffalo. "I contacted a game reserve in South Dakota. They informed me that they supplied buffalo free of charge to zoos and other such organizations. They did on occasion give buffalos to individuals," stated Baird. It turned out that this buffalo source was not for him. "They have strict requirements on care of their animals. Periodically they come to your farm and inspect the buffalo. I would rather own the buffalo and be able to do with them as I please," explained Baird.

Don Baird's search for a buffalo trader continued until last year when he saw the following ad in Progressive Farmer: *Buffalo. Will Deliver. Warren Van Hook, West Point, IN 47992. Phone 317-538-3282.*

Baird contacted Van Hook the very night that he read the ad. "He informed me that he had a buffalo delivery to make in Memphis. Since my farm was on his way he said that he would deliver them free of charge," said Baird. Van Hook became ill and was unable to deliver them at the appointed time. Don Baird traveled to West Point, Indiana and visited Van Hook and his buffalo.

"He had a bull that stood well above my head and weighed about 3,000 pounds. He had five or six bulls running together and they seemed to get along fine. His fence consisted of only strands of barb wire," said Baird.

"Van Hook explained that he raised buffalo in an attempt to get the population of the buffalo up. He sells all of his calves every year and has buyers all over the country. Whenever one of his buffalo dies, the head is stuffed and sold for about $300. Even the feet are stuffed and wind up as ash trays. On the floor of Van Hook's house was a rug made from the hide of a buffalo that died when it was very young. About the only part of the buffalo that is not used is the tail."

Baird returned home and awaited the fulfillment of his dream. Shortly before Christmas last year a gooseneck trailer, that was heavily reinforced, pulled into the drive of the Baird home. On board were a yearling bull, a two-year-old bull and a bred five year-old cow. "That was our Christmas gift," said Don's wife, Marilyn.

The buffalo immediately made themselves at home and Baird began trying to train the yearling bull, Sam. He eventually became able to place a saddle on the animal's back. "I could rub him all over and he didn't mind a bit. Buffalo must be a one person animal because whenever my boys would approach me and the yearling, the animal would turn and run," stated Baird. "I began to wonder about the possible danger of his horns so I contacted Dr. Wempe who eventually dehorned him. After he was dehorned you could look down in there and see his brain. I thought I had better not mess with him until he healed. Later I got busy farming and haven't had time to try to train him since," added Baird.

"The meanest one of the three is the cow. Van Hook warned me that I had better not fasten up the cow with the bull. He said the cow would probably hurt the bull. The bull runs in my field and don't offer to hurt anything."

The two-year-old bull is known as Geronimo.

Don Baird presently has the cow, which is affectionately known as Big Mama, in a pen by herself. "Many people stop to look at the buffalo. They often step up to the fence to look at the cow. Sometimes she turns her head and horns toward them. Almost always the people jump back. Buffalo are bluffers. Usually if you stand your ground they won't do a thing. They are only mean when they know you are afraid of them."

"It is hard to keep your feet still when the cow lurches at you. The cow bosses the bulls and always eats first. She is liberated," added Marilyn Baird.

According to Baird, the age of a buffalo is determined by the animal's horns. "At first they (the horns) are straight. As the buffalo gets older they start turning. Buffalo do not mature until about two years old. It is very unusual for a cow any younger to have a calf."

Buffalo cows have a strong maternal instinct. Baird indicated that he has been told that a buffalo cow will reject her calf if it is touched by a human during its first three days of life. The cow is very protective of the calf and quite adequately protects it from outsiders. Baird's cow should calve within the next couple of months. "The way the cow is built it is hard to tell is she is going to have a calf. About the only real way to tell is by the udder which becomes swollen in the latter stages of pregnancy. The buffalo cow's udder is similar to that of a horse," said Baird.

Shortly after purchasing the buffalo, Baird purchased

some Angus cattle which he hopes to cross with the buffalo. At present Baird is uncertain as to what kind of results he can expect from his attempts at crossbreeding.

Breeding buffalo with cattle is not a new idea. Several years ago, when it was first attempted, the resulting animal was referred to as a "cattalo." Difficulties of producing the "cattalo" were at first twofold. Male offspring of the first generation are usually sterile. A reliable fertile bull is usually not produced until the sixth generation. The other problem was the high death rate of the calves.

"I have been told that the "beefalo" ("cattalo" is no longer used by buffalo breeders) is sterile. I can't completely believe this because I have seen "beefalo" semen advertised for sale," stated Baird.

"Buffalo calves are usually smaller than other calves. For this reason I plan on crossing an Angus bull with the buffalo cow. I shouldn't have any calving problems such as those that some present beef breeders have." (Many beef breeders produce calves that are too large for the mother cow to deliver.)

"If the crossbreeding works out I may add more buffalo to my herd. At present, an organization in Virginia is trying to organize 'beefalo' producers," said Baird.

The "beefalo" is a much larger animal that the progenitors of either side. The fur makes fine robes and they are very hardy animals. They can withstand the bitter cold of winter and have been known to survive in weather fifty degrees below zero, without artificial food or shelter. Many experts believe that "beefalo" are the coming thing.

"My buffalo eat the same feed as my cattle. In fact, they will eat hay that the cattle will not touch. I have a shelter available for them, sometimes they use it and sometimes they don't. Van Hook, who lives farther north, never shelters his buffalo," stated Baird.

A buffalo is an extremely heavy animal with a massive head, short neck, short curved horns, and a high hump on its shoulder. A full grown bull may stand from 5 feet 6 inches to about six feet tall. The female is smaller and usually weighs about 800 pounds as compared to 1,800 to 2,400 pounds for the bull.

"When I first got the buffalo I weighed the yearling and the bull at the stockyard. The bull weighed 975 pounds and the yearling weighed about 525 pounds," said Baird. "I got a few stares at the stockyard," he added.

Buffalo do not "moo" like cattle. Rather, they make a strange grunting sound. At different times of the year the animals participate in what is known as the buffalo dance. During this "dance" the buffalo run stiff-legged while growling and belching all the way,

"I had the buffalo put up once and when I let them out they went crazy. I don't know if you would call it a dance but it sure was weird," said Baird.

"In the winter, whenever there is a change in the weather, the buffalo go crazy. You can tell when something is going to happen by watching the buffalo," added Marilyn.

"The closest other buffalo that I know of are in Carmi, Illinois. There used to be some in Madisonville but I don't know if they are still there. There are some in the Land Between the Lakes but they are not owned by an individual," said Baird.

The American bison is not a true buffalo but is continued to be called buffalo by the general public. The buffalo has 14 pairs of ribs as compared to 13 for cattle. Cattle have over 50 different blood types while the buffalo has only one.

At one time over 50 million buffalo roamed the United States and Canada. In 1800 all buffalo were eliminated from the area east of the Mississippi. It was realized shortly afterwards that bison meat and hide were of commercial value. Hide hunters, butchers, and tongue picklers began widespread exploitation of the animal.

The Canadian bison disappeared around 1800. The opening of the Union Pacific and Kansas Pacific railroads around 1865 almost brought about the extinction of the American bison.

By 1900 almost 50 million buffalo had been slaughtered by careless hunters. The buffalo faced extinction. In 1905 the American Bison Society was formed to try and save the buffalo. Through the society's efforts a few hundred buffalo were saved. Around 1970 the United States and Canadian population of buffalo was estimated at 30,000.

To many the buffalo is an oddity, a curiosity only narrowly saved from extinction. To Don Baird, and others like him, the buffalo has a great future. One day the buffalo may again flourish in great numbers with its head held high greeting those who come to stare.

OK, identify the basic elements of the story. Tell me who would care about the story. And, perhaps most importantly, tell me what I

don't like about this story and would change.
Does the lead work? Would you change it in any way? Should there have been additional sources?
(Again, you'll find my comments about this story in Appendix B.)

Do you like Fords or Chevys?

Let's look at another story. This story appeared in Kentuckiana Show 'n Go, a car magazine published by Landmark Community Newspapers. It was the cover story for the premiere issue.

I was the publisher of the magazine for about two years prior to its cancellation. At the same time, I was also news editor for the Central Kentucky News-Journal.

Doing both jobs at the same time kept me busy.

I wrote the following story and took the photographs that accompanied it in the magazine.

He drives a Ford, she drives a Chevy
Together they find happiness at car shows and cruises

Traveling through a small town near Atlanta last spring while giving out Gideon Bibles, Don Green noticed a red 1957 Chevrolet coupe with a "for sale" sign stuck in the window.

Green stopped, kicked the tires, looked under the hood and asked the price.

Though he wasn't pleased with the recent paint job applied to the classic car, money soon changed hands.

"It was in my price range," Green said of the '57 Chevy.

After sealing the deal, Green made arrangements to return to Atlanta so he could drive the car home to Campbellsville.

Green readily admits the Chevrolet isn't his. It belongs to his wife Sue.

While it wouldn't be quite accurate to say Green doesn't like Chevrolets, he does prefer Fords. His favorite ride is a 1963 ½ Ford Galaxie 500 which he has had for about four years.

"I always wanted one," Green said. "My folks owned one and I drove it as a teenager."

Green's car is black with a red interior and his wife's is red with a black interior.

The Galaxie outmuscles the Chevrolet in the engine compartment. It has a 350-cubic-inch engine with a two-barrel carb while the '57 has a 283 with a four barrel.

Both have automatic transmissions – the Ford's is called a Cruise-O-Matic while the Chevrolet's is known as a Hydramatic.

Both cars are driven regularly.

Green said he bought the cars to enjoy, not restore to better than new condition. If he needs a loaf of bread or a gallon of milk, he doesn't hesitate to hop in one of the classic cars for a trip to the grocery.

The cars are also driven rain or shine, summer or winter.

"These are original drivers," Green said. "I call them my cruising cars."

Many might be hesitant to drive the cars on such a regular basis.

"There are two breeds of us," Green said of classic car enthusiasts. "One likes to look at them. I want to drive them."

The Galaxie is in better condition than the 1957 Chevrolet and Green does plan some modest improvements. Either, he said, would make a good show car should he someday decide to do a more complete restoration.

Green's primary concern is the mechanical condition of the cars.

"I don't let these babies stay parked," Green said. "There's no place I wouldn't drive them."

Regularly, Green drives the Chevrolet to a cruise in Bardstown which always attracts hundreds of cars.

Sometimes he drives the Ford.

Both cars are almost 100 percent original. And what's not original, Green said, is slowly being returned to the way it was when the cars rolled off the assembly line.

The Galaxie has a set of custom wheels as well as a set of original wheels.

In the past, Green has entered the car in several shows, winning a number of trophies. He always enters an original class and puts on his original wheels for show purposes.

As soon as he's back home though, the custom wheels go back on.

Green said the Galaxie isn't identical to the car his parents had in Lancaster, S.C. That car was red with a black interior and had a high performance 390 cubic-inch engine with a four-speed.

"My Dad never could figure out why I couldn't keep tires on the car," Green said.

Driving his Galaxie, though, rekindles memories even if it isn't identical to the one he drove as a teenager.

Green found the Galaxie in Flint, Mich. where he worked for AC Spark Plug. He is the third owner of the car.

After purchasing the car, Green learned the original owner was a good friend of his who had stored it for a few years while waiting for his son to return from Vietnam.

The son was killed in Vietnam, though, and the car ultimately was sold to the man Green bought it from in essentially the condition it is in now.

The Galaxie has 68,000 miles on the odometer and the Chevrolet shows almost 87,000.

Green said the Galaxie attracts more attention at car shows and cruises than the Chevrolet.

There were a large number of 1957 Chevrolets produced, Green said, and there are usually quite a few at shows and cruises.

"The Ford gets more reactions," Green said. "It's more unusual."

The fact Green drives a Ford and his wife drives a Chevrolet has been the subject of some good-natured kidding.

"I joke with her," Green said. "I tell her the Ford is the better of the two cars but hers cost the most.

"She doesn't say much."

Green retired two years ago and he and his wife moved from Michigan to Crawford Street in Campbellsville.

That's a move that's not all that difficult for Green to explain.

In Michigan, Dr. Randy Davenport was music director at the church the Greens attended. The Rev. James Hatfield was minister.

Davenport came to Campbellsville to become president at the college. Hatfield also came to Campbellsville to continue his ministry. The Greens followed. It just took them longer to get there.

Green is still involved with the Gideons and sometimes drives one of his classic cars while handing out Bibles. He's also a member of the Tri-County Car Club.

Green said his interest in classic cars is also easy to explain.

"Driving them brings back many good memories," Green said. "I have newer vehicles, but it's fun to drive the older cars and remember what it used to be like."

Now that you've read the story, identify all of the basic elements. Also, look at the detail included and consider how it adds to the story. Does the lead work? Would you change it in any way? Should there have been additional sources?

Consider the angle of this story – Ford vs. Chevrolet, husband vs. wife. Is it appropriate? Is it written in a humorous way that would offend no one?

Who would be interested in this story? Would only classic car lovers read it?

You'll also find my observations about this story in Appendix B.

Appendix A
How to remain in the good graces of your editor and/or readers

—Meet your deadlines. Deadlines are not optional. They do not apply to everyone except you. Missing deadlines disrupts the production schedule and causes extra work for the editor and anyone else who handles your story between the time it is turned in and appears in print. If you plan to work in journalism, public relations or any other form of mass media, you will meet your deadlines. Period.

—If you make an appointment to interview someone, be on time. Never be late. If anything, be early.

—Understand your story before you begin writing. It is impossible to convey the message of the story if you don't know what it is.

—Learn the stylebook. Most publications use the Associated Press Stylebook. Most have copies of the stylebook available. Understand when you use 101 Main St. and Main Street. Understand when you use February and Feb. 10.

—A sentence must contain a complete thought and must have a subject and a verb. Sentence fragments. Are confusing. To the editors. And to the readers.

—Check all spelling especially of names, festivals, etc. Also make certain that you have a person's title correct. Don't be afraid to ask. It is better to ask than make a mistake. People can forgive many mistakes. Few, however, can get over their name being spelled incorrectly.

—Read your story after it is finished. Read it aloud. Let someone else read it before the editor sees it. Do you understand each and every sentence? Is each and every sentence clear? Does your story answer every possible question?

—"I" and "me" do not belong in stories. "I" and "me" are only acceptable in columns. Only the most experienced writers write columns. Unless you are specifically told otherwise, you are not writing a column. "I" and "me" do not belong. Take them out if they are in your story. The story is not about you or your opinions. A reporter is a conduit for information. Your opinions, thoughts and observations DO NOT belong in a story.

—You may include opinions or thoughts of others but they must be properly attributed. For example, do not say: "Sam felt bad." That is your conclusion. Instead, say, "Sam said he felt bad." There IS a big difference.

—Only commonly accepted facts require no attribution. If it is spring, you probably do not have to attribute a statement that grass is green. Statements that are not commonly accepted fact (and that's the majority of what you will have in your stories) MUST be attributed. The word "said" is almost always the proper term to use when identifying the source or a statement.

—Verify all of your "facts." We are in the business of telling the truth. If there is any doubt, check it out.

—Avoid redundancies. It is absolutely necessary that on each and every story reporters list only the true facts. You must be reasonable and fair, plain and simple and put the honest truth first and foremost in your stories.

There are seven redundancies in the last two sentences. Can you find them?

—Do you know what time it is? You might be writing a story on Monday about something that happened last Friday. Your story is due Thursday and will appear in next Wednesday's newspaper. If you say in your story that something happened on Monday, will the editor or reader know what day you are talking about?

Keep in mind when the story will appear. State times, dates, etc. in such a way that readers are not confused.

—Don't tell readers what questions you asked to get the statements that are in your story. The question that was asked generally is obvious.

Don't say: When asked why the new leash law is important, the city council member said, "It is important that the council pass this law so residents can walk their streets without fear of being attacked by dogs."

Simply say: "It is important that the council pass this law so residents can walk their streets without fear of being attacked by dogs," the council member said.

—Is the lead as written really the lead? Does it tell the reader why he or she should care? Know your readers and know what matters to them.

In the first sentence or two, it should be clear to the readers why they must reader farther. If it is not, rewrite your story.

—Do not permit your sources to edit (or read) your stories. Many may wish to read your story after it is finished. Do not allow it. They may wish to change their quotes, the lead, even the focus of the story.

It is also not fair to permit them to see what others have said. That would be especially true if the story is controversial.

If a source asks before the interview is over to review a question or two to ensure you understood what was said, that is OK.

Allowing sources to read a completed story slows and changes the production process. It may also change the "truth." It is NEVER a good idea.

—Above all, read your story after you believe it is finished. Is it easy to read and are all sentences clear? If you don't understand something or stumble here and there, your readers will too.

Remember, none of us are perfect writers. We all need editing. Never take what an editor says personally. An editor's job is to clean up what we failed to. An editor is the last set of eyes between you and the readers.

Appendix B
My thoughts on "your turn"

What's wrong with the story about Donald Baird and his buffalo? It's too long. The lengthy history of the buffalo at the end of the story should be eliminated. There might be some information that could be worked into the story, such as the fact the buffalo once faced extinction. The majority of the history, though, needs to go.

That alone would make the story considerably shorter.

"Said" is the only word that should be used for attribution. Some of the quotes are too long and unnecessary. Much of the information used in quote marks could be paraphrased, if it's important to the story.

A story should be much more than a series of quotes strung together. Use your sources exact words only when they are the best way to tell the story. Quote that which is quotable.

The end of the story is a little "pie in the sky" for me. Yes, I wrote it. As an experienced writer, editor and reader, I would never end a story that way today. As written, it includes my opinion. It's also a bit pretentious:

"One day the buffalo may again flourish in great numbers with its head held high greeting those who come to stare."

Who was I trying to impress? This wasn't a story about a cure for cancer or the discovery of ultimate truth. It was about a man raising buffalo.

Let's turn to the story about the man who owns a Ford who is married to a woman who drives a Chevrolet.

I like the story. It never won an award. It didn't generate many comments. But I think it's much better written than the buffalo story which did win a second-place award from the Kentucky Press Association.

The story is light. There's very little that's serious about it. (It is the absolute truth, though.) It's intended to entertain and, perhaps, bring a smile to the face of the reader. If it did that, I'm happy.

Some of our stories will enlighten, inform and perhaps change our world for the better. Some may do no more than provide a moment's escape for the reader from his daily troubles. That's OK with me.

Appendix C
Reporters often must be photographers

If you're a reporter for a small publication, you're also a photographer. That's just the way it is. Some newspapers are, in fact, so small that there's one editor and one reporter – the same person.

That person likely is also the photographer.

At the Sturgis News, I was a reporter, a photographer, a graphic artist, a bookkeeper and once even helped the owner pour concrete to solve a flooding problem.

Even when I was an editor at a twice-weekly newspaper, I was also a photographer.

It simply makes sense to send one person to cover a story. That means that person must be capable of conducting an interview, writing the story and taking photographs.

Why pay two people or more when you can pay one?

Don't let any of that bother you. I enjoy taking photographs. Writing the story and taking the photographs also gives you more control over the final product. If you're also the editor, you may have complete control over what readers actually see.

Originally, this book was to contain a chapter on photography. I quickly discovered that a thorough explanation of photography could not be contained within one chapter. It will take an entire book to pass on just the basics.

Get yourself a digital camera that accepts interchangeable lenses. Buy a good quality wide angle lens and the best telephoto lens you can afford. Learn all you can about them. Look for a camera with a resolution of at least five megapixels.

Read all you can about photography. Practice, practice, practice. Look closely at your work. What looks good? What doesn't? Keep taking photos until you get it right. With a digital camera, you won't be wasting film, and you'll become a better photographer.

While some of us may be better photographers than others, anyone should be able to take at least an acceptable photograph. You have to know some basics and practice, practice, practice.

That's also true of writing, isn't it?

Another word of advice, keep copies of your photos and stories. That's easy to do in today's digital world. On a regular basis, save your digital photos and an electronic version of your stories onto a CD.

If you want to keep actual copies of stories and photos, that's fine. Just be aware of how much space that will require in a few years.

Someday you will want copies of your work. Make sure you have them.

Some final thoughts

Being a reporter can indeed be the best job in the world. It can also be the worst, all in the same day, perhaps in the same hour.

You deal with people when they are at their best. You deal with people when they are at their worst. You share their hopes and dreams. You laugh and cry with them. You share their tragedies.

A good reporter must love people. A good reporter must care about the community and have faith that tomorrow can indeed be better. A good reporter, I believe, must have faith in God and truly keep in mind the Golden Rule.

"Do unto others as you would have them do unto you."

Reporters face ethical dilemmas on a regular basis. Many are difficult to reconcile. Look inside yourself to determine what is right and just.

Write stories that matter. Write stories that interest people. While you must have a world view, you must also focus on what is of most importance and interest to those who share the community you call home. Keep your stories local, keeping in mind that the definition of local varies depending on the audience for your particular publication.

For most non-daily newspapers, that's the boundary of the county in which you live.

That's also why as far as reporters are concerned, their world has to end at the county line.

About the author

Stan McKinney is an assistant professor of journalism at Campbellsville University in Campbellsville, Ky.

He has a bachelor of science degree in journalism with a minor in chemistry and a master of science degree in communication with journalism emphasis from Murray State University.

McKinney is a native of Princeton, Ky. where he graduated from high school in 1970. His parents, Norvell and Gurtha May McKinney, still live in Princeton.

Mckinney was a reporter and photographer for the Sturgis News in Sturgis, Ky. from 1975 to 1976. He moved from there to Shelbyville, Ky. where he was a reporter and photographer for The Sentinel-News for a little more than three years.

The Sentinel-News is owned by Landmark Community Newspapers Inc. The company promoted him in 1980 to news editor at the Central Kentucky News-Journal in Campbellsville, Ky.

In 1987, McKinney began teaching as an adjunct professor at Campbellsville University. He left the newspaper business in the fall of 2000 and became a full-time professor.

McKinney teaches a variety of courses including Reporting and Newswriting, Advanced Reporting and Newswriting, Photojournalism, Advanced Photojournalism, Mass Media Law, Desktop Publishing, Graphics, Public Relations and Advanced Public Relations.

During his newspaper career, McKinney covered school boards, fiscal courts, city councils, zoning boards and all other types of public meetings. He has been to Atlantic City, N.J. three times for the Miss America Pageant and once to South Padre Island, Texas for the Miss USA Pageant.

He followed a high school group to France for a series of stories and photos on a possible Sister City relationship with Les Andelys, France and Campbellsville.

McKinney has written all types of news stories, features, editorials and columns during his more than 25 years in the newspaper business. For 21 years, he wrote a weekly column.

At the Central Kentucky News-Journal, McKinney designed and laid out the front page for more than two decades.

He also served as publisher for a specialty magazine, Kentuckiana Show 'n Go, devoted to show cars in Kentucky and Indiana. For almost two years, he wrote a monthly column for the magazine as well as other

Stan McKinney poses with his 2003 Mustang Mach 1 during the 40th Anniversary of the Mustang Show sponsored by the Mustang Club of America in April 2004. His car received an Award of Merit during the show which attracted more than 4,000 Mustangs.

stories. He also took many of the photos for the magazine and did much of the layout.

He has had stories and photos published in various newspapers and magazines.

McKinney was one of the editors and a featured photographer in "Images from the Heartland," a photography book about Campbellsville and Taylor County. His photography has also been featured in other books.

For several years, McKinney has been chair of the Campbellsville Fourth of July Celebration. He has been a member of various civic clubs including the Campbellsville Kiwanis Club and the Tri-County Car Club.

He has been a member of the Society of Professional Journalists, the Kentucky Newspaper Photographers Associations and the National Newspaper Photographers Association.

The Kentucky Press Association, the Society of Professional

Journalists and Landmark Community Newspapers Inc. have honored McKinney numerous times with awards for photography, writing and design.

The Kentucky School Board Association in 1981 honored McKinney as educational reporter of the year. The Campbellsville/Taylor County Chamber of Commerce named him as Citizen of the Year in 1992.

Campbellsville University in 1996 selected McKinney as Adjunct Professor of the Year.

In 2002, McKinney was elected to Campbellsville City Council. He has also served on the parks board and the tree board in Campbellsville.

Photography is one of McKinney's hobbies. He enjoys photographing a variety of subjects including flowers he grows in his own garden.

Mustangs of all years are also of special interest to McKinney. He owns a candyapple red 1966 Mustang convertible with a white top and a torch red 2003 Mustang Mach 1. He is a member of the Mustang Club of America and has shown his cars at a variety of shows all across the country.

McKinney's wife, Joan Cottongim McKinney, is director of university communications at Campbellsville University. She also has a newspaper background and has worked at the Danville (Ky.) Advocate-Messenger and The Sentinel-News where they met.

They have a daughter, Calen, who works part-time at the Central Kentucky News-Journal and is a communication student at Campbellsville University.

The McKinneys are also cat lovers and have long shared their home with their four-legged friends.

In addition to raising flowers, McKinney is also an avid water gardener. He has built two ponds and two fountains in the last five years.

McKinney is continuing his studies. He is completing a program in digital imaging through the New York Institute of Photography. He also plans a book on photojournalism.